AuthorHelp.Net presents

Write Your Novel:

First Page to First Draft

By Tom Holbrook

and the staff of AuthorHelp.net

Write Your Novel: First Page to First Draft
Copyright 2022 by Tom Holbrook
All Rights Reserved, though you are free to steal any good ideas
you find, because that's what artists do!

Published by Piscataqua Press
32 Daniel St., Portsmouth, NH 03801

Visit www.AuthorHelp.net

Stock image from Shutterstock: linktr.ee/abstract412

ISBN: 9781958669099

Write Your Novel:

First Page to First Draft

Table of Contents

Part One:
Preparation is Key

Chapter 1: The Rabbit Hole!

The conflict at the heart of all stories, and of all humans (including writers), is the battle between fear and desire.[i]

You have decided you want to write a book. Outstanding! *Desire!*

Maybe you've already tried. Maybe you've written Chapter One, and then rewritten it, and then rewritten it, and then looked for typos, and then checked the word count, and then checked the word count again. But you never went on to Chapter Two. *Fear!*

What to do? Well, if you're like many people, you go down the rabbit hole.

Don't go down the Rabbit Hole!!

Research is admirable. Writing is an ancient craft, and you can find volumes and volumes of excellent instruction and inspiration. Before you begin your novel, you might want to go online and do a little research into Story Structure, Indie vs. Traditional Publishing, Passive Voice, The Hero's Journey, The Virgin's Quest, Scrivener, Pomodoro Method, etc., Etc., ETC!!!!!!!!!

Don't do it! Not yet anyway.

Researching writing techniques and the publishing landscape can be a rabbit hole of epic proportions. I know because I've gone down it. And some day, you will, too. It's irresistible. But our priority *right now* is to get you from the first page to the completed first draft. The second book in the Author Help series will take you from your first draft to your final draft. At that point, you can do all the research you like: read all the books, watch all the YouTubers, take all the online courses, give your manuscript to Beta readers or agents. But if you start down that rabbit hole now, your chances of getting that first draft written will plummet.

"But wait," I hear you saying. "Tom, if I ignore all that information, how am I going to write a brilliant book?"

There are two answers to that question:

1) You're *not* going to write a brilliant book. Not yet. You're going to write a first draft. What is often elegantly referred to as your "Vomit Draft." Because here's a secret: getting to the end is the hardest part. Or, as has often been said, "You can't edit a blank page."

In this book, I'm going to give you the fundamentals of story and character that you need to get started, and lots of encouragement and guideposts along the way as you write your first draft. You will overcome what Steven Pressfield calls Resistance and vomit that first draft out. What's Resistance? Who's Steven Pressfield? Don't look it up! *Rabbit Hole alert, Rabbit Hole alert!!*

2) You are going to *trust me.*

Why should you trust me? Fair question.

I'm an editor and publisher, and for the past twenty years I've owned a small bookstore. I've also written six novels under a pen name with more on the way. My books all have one thing in common — they started with a completed first draft.

As an editor and publisher, I have made first-time authors my niche, and I have helped over 150 authors independently publish their first book. Developmental editing, proofreading, cover design, blurbs, websites, Facebook ads — I've done a bit of everything.

And, I've gone down the rabbit hole. I've taken courses, read dozens of books, listened to hundreds of hours of podcasts about writing, editing, publishing, and marketing. In this book, I've brought together the best ideas I've found, simplified them as much as possible, and blended them into a system for getting your first draft done.

It all comes down to that rabbit hole. Twenty different people could write this guidebook (and dozens have) and send you down twenty different paths. And all of them might be righteous paths. They might all help you get that first draft written, which is of course the entire point. But if you read all of them, you're apt to get stuck.

So, why use my system? Why read *this* book? Because it will work for *most* people. It's comprehensive without being too complex. And it's focused on you, the first-time author.

P.S. You don't have to be a first-time author to read this book and get useful ideas out of it. The method I've laid out might be just the thing you need to make it easier to get through your second book, or your thirtieth.

How This Book Will Work

Great, you're still reading. I'm going to tell you about how I organized this book, and how you will use it, and then we'll get to work. While I try to keep everything as simple as possible, there is still structure, strategy, and accountability built into this method.

As I've mentioned, I've done a huge amount of research into the craft of writing. I'll be using bits and pieces from everywhere, like the magpie I am, to build a plan for you to get the draft done.

At its most basic, your story needs **characters**, a **conflict**, and a

plot. In that order! Yes, I know that you already have an idea for your plot, and you probably know a lot about your main character already, and that's great. But before you begin, we need to nail down your **story.**

Wait, aren't story and plot the same thing? No, they aren't. Plot is used to reveal story. A *story* tells the reader about a character dealing with a conflict they can't avoid, and the **internal** change they have to make to overcome that conflict. The *plot* is the details you've created to bring that story to life. The plot is the **external** happenings of the book. Story: *Internal.* Plot: *External.*

Here's an example:

Story: A disadvantaged young person, after a strange encounter, must overcome their self-doubt and innocence to save the new, larger world of romance and adventure they have come to embrace.

Possible Plot A: When Luke Skywalker intercepts a message from a leader of the galactic rebellion, he enters a new and dangerous world, where finding the confidence to wield an ancient power is his only hope to save his friends and maybe the entire galaxy.

Possible Plot B: When Wall-E, a small garbage droid on the uninhabitable planet Earth, meets Eva, a sophisticated robot on a mysterious quest, he must leave his simple life on Earth behind and learn to navigate a new, high-tech world in order to help Eva complete a five-hundred-year-old mission to bring human life back to Earth.

You could say that both *Star Wars* and *Wall-E* have the same story but very different plots. Get it? Good, because I'll come back again and again to that question: **What internal story are you trying to tell?**

We are going to find the bones of your story by exploring your character, theme, and plot ideas, and then we are going to set up **Five Tentpole Scenes** to build your novel on. We'll use that information to describe the story you are trying to tell, first as a **Pixar Pitch**, and then as a **Logline** (sometimes called an elevator pitch). Then, you are going to write. And write, and write.

How long is it going to take? That's up to you, of course. **However, with the step-by-step system I've set up, and two hours of writing a day, you should be able to finish your first draft in ten weeks. The prep work of Part One, at two hours a day, should take you about ten days.** Obviously, YMMV (Don't look it up! It means "Your mileage may vary").

Does that seem like more time than you can commit in a day? That's okay. Two hours is the sweet spot, but if you can only commit to one hour a day, then work with what you've got. Half an hour? Sure, but now, of course, you are looking at 40 weeks instead of 10.

Think the opposite is true? Think you can sit down at your desk every night and write for three or four hours? Well, more power to you. Just remember, it's consistency that will help you win the race. No matter how little, or how much, just try to do *some* work every day.

Back to how this book will work: First, we'll talk about the five important scenes your story must have. I call them the **Five Tentpole Scenes** because they prop up your manuscript. You will decide, before you write, what is going to happen in those scenes (don't worry, they aren't set in stone). Then, we'll use character sheets to make sure each of your major characters has clear **wants**, **needs**, and **flaws**, as well as a distinctive **voice** all their own.

Next, we'll use this preliminary work to form an outline cheat sheet. Do you think you're **a Plotter** — the type of writer who likes a detailed outline — or are you a "**Pantser**," (an affectionate term for an author who writes by the seat of their pants)? In this book, you'll be using the Five Tentpole Scene method, which lands right in between the two.

The last important thing I'll teach you before you get started is the anatomy of a scene. You build your novel scene by scene by scene, so you must know how to make a scene work. Spoiler alert: *Every scene needs the same thing* — **Conflict, Choice, and Consequence.**[ii] If you know where your scene takes place, who is in your scene, what they want, and what the conflict is, you'll find writing quicker and easier.

Then (finally!) the writing begins in Part Two! You'll start out at 500 words per day (that's about one to two pages of text) as you write your way to the first Tentpole. After that, your pace will increase, because you will know how to build a scene, and you'll know the direction to the next Tentpole.

After you read each chapter of this book, you'll go off and write several scenes, and then return for the next chapter, making your way through the manuscript. (If you want to read through this entire book first, that's fine, but then read it again as you do your actual drafting.)

Easy, right? Not really. Just like your protagonist, you'll be faced with self-doubt and seemingly overwhelming obstacles. You'll discover your **Flaw** (Netflix!! Sudoku!! Sleep!!) and fight to overcome it. And you'll succeed because the entire time you will use your personal theme as your compass. And your personal theme is this: *My protagonist is important to me. They are on an emotional journey, and I, the author, am the only one who can see them through it.*

Okay, let's get started...

Chapter 2: The Five Tentpole Scenes

Your protagonist is on an emotional journey, and you, the author, are the only one who can see them through it. You need to give them a strong support system to hang their story on. The Five Tentpoles.

The first two Tentpole Scenes are the **Inciting Incident** and the **No Turning Back Scene.** These two scenes are part of the First Act of your book, which in terms of volume is generally the first 25% of your novel.

The third Tentpole Scene is the **Midpoint Tentpole Scene**, which takes place smack in the middle of Act Two of your book, which accounts for the middle 50% of your novel.

The Third and final act, which makes up the last 25% of your book, will contain the **Choice Tentpole Scene** and the **Finale Tentpole Scene.**

Umm, Tom, what do tents have to do with anything?

The term Tentpole Scene is one I made up, and it's simply an easy way to look at story structure. And that's our goal, right? To keep it simple so we don't get hung up. Believe me, there are *many* complicated ways to look at story structure. Some of the most well known in the publishing and screenwriting worlds are *The Story Grid*, *Save the Cat*, and *The Hero's Journey*. Some favorites in the indie author community are the *Three Story Method* by Thorn and Bohannon and Libby Hawker's *Take Off Your Pants*. But guess what? We will not talk about them right now!

Are you sensing a theme in my writing? You should be, because it's the point of this book: *Don't go down the rabbit hole! Keep it simple!*

If we are keeping it so simple, why do you need to learn about story structure? Shouldn't you just write the best you can and worry about that stuff later?

No. Because **when you get stuck in your writing, it's usually because of a lack of story structure.** You've written yourself into a corner or out into a vast, dry desert and you abandon your novel because you can't figure out which way to go. Understanding the very basics of story structure will keep you going when you get stuck. The best way to keep your story from collapsing — like a broken tent — is to have a series of well-spaced support poles holding it up. Doing this work ahead of time will save you pain, anguish, and wasted words during the drafting process.

In its simplest form, a story has a beginning, a middle, and an end. These happen to be three of our Five Tentpole Scenes. The beginning is the *Inciting Incident Tentpole*, the middle is the *Midpoint Tentpole*, and the end is the *Finale Tentpole*. In between these scenes, let's add the *Point of No Return Tentpole* and the *Choice Tentpole*, and we'll have our Five Tentpole Scenes.

You know who's *superb* at story? Pixar. That company has consistently produced dozens of remarkable stories over the last twenty years. How do they do it?

One factor is how they approach story. There's something called the Pixar Pitch, attributed to the masterminds from that company. The idea is that we can boil any story down to this pitch:

Every day...
One day ...
Because of that...
Because of that...
Until finally...

Can you make your story idea fit that pitch? Because if you can, you almost have your Five Tentpole Scenes already! Write your pitch, then look for your Tentpole Scenes in it. Don't worry, it'll probably change anyway, but it's a good exercise. If you can't make your story fit that pitch, that's okay; we'll come back to this after we talk about building characters in Chapter 3 and that will help. But right now, let's inspect each Tentpole.

Tentpole One: Inciting incident

Every day, Wall-E processed trash on an abandoned Earth. He collected things he found interesting, and he learned about love and emotions from watching old videos and listening to old music. One day, he found a tiny living plant amongst the waste.

Boom! That's your Inciting Incident. Everything else in the movie springs from this point.

Simply, the Inciting Incident takes your **protagonist** out of their daily grind and into a world of emotional conflict. It doesn't matter what genre you write in, a powerful story will be about change. And while it will ultimately be about a change in your protagonist, it usually starts with a change in external circumstances. That's your Inciting Incident. Ideally, it happens in the first 5-15% of your book. While it's important to set up the normal world of your protagonist so that the reader can really feel the change, you can't wait too long for your Inciting Incident or your reader will get bored.

This is an enormous danger with genres that require a lot of world building, like science fiction or fantasy. You may want to spend pages describing how hobbits live their lives before getting around to the bit where Frodo and friends leave the Shire, but if you do, your reader will get bored. (Oops, did I say that out loud? Sorry Tolkien fans...). Worldbuilding is tricky, but we'll get to that later.

Tentpole Two: Point of No Return

So, your protagonist's life is rolling along and then boom! Inciting Incident. What happens next? Some characters will try to ignore the change, others will run off totally unprepared. Some protagonists will be directly affected; others will confront a terrible situation for someone they love.

Maybe someone makes the protagonist an offer they can't refuse, and maybe they refuse it. Maybe the guy who helps you change your flat tire is cute, but yuck, he's also conceited. My point is, just because the Inciting Incident has happened, you will still want some brilliant scenes before you get to the Point of No Return. These scenes will reveal your character and their flaw, introduce new characters and subplots, and help build your fictional world.

But eventually, and hopefully around 25% of the way into your book, you will reach the Point of No Return. This is the point where, because of the Inciting Incident, the status quo just won't hold anymore. Something must be done, and once that journey starts, it must be very difficult, near impossible, to turn back. Or, as the Pixar Pitch says,

"Because of that..."

In an action story, like *Captain America*, this would be when Steve Rogers takes the serum that will turn him into a super soldier. It's irreversible, and if it doesn't work will probably kill him. There's no returning from that!

In a more character driven or romantic story, like *Jane Eyre*, this would be when Jane leaves her staid teaching job to take a position as a governess at the mysterious Thornfield Hall, because she believes she has more to offer the world than she can in her current situation. Now, if things went terribly wrong, Jane could probably return to teaching, but it would be a huge emotional setback.

And of course, in *The Wizard of Oz*, it's when Dorothy takes the red pill instead of the blue pill. No, wait, that's *The Matrix*. You get the idea, though, right?

The last thing I'll say about this Tentpole: If you really want to make your global story work, *it has to be your character's decision* to step through the gate and onto the yellow brick road. Often, something happens to the character that makes it impossible to turn back. Even then, it's better if that something is the character's fault. Are there exceptions to this? Sure (see: *The Martian*). But they are hard to pull off. And, seeing as this is probably your first book, let's keep on the simple path.

Tentpole Three: Midpoint

Wow, the middle of the book is hard. You thought figuring out the grand finale would be the hard part, or maybe coming up with the perfect character to express your theme. Nope. It's what's often called the messy middle. And I'll be honest, it can be a slog.

The Midpoint Tentpole Scene will come after you've spent an enjoyable time throwing complication after complication at your protagonist and introducing great new characters and crafting subplots. It will come at when you look at your word count and think: How can I only be at 30,000 words? I want this book to be 60,000 words! What do I do between now and the Finale? We'll get to that, and if we do a good job with our Midpoint Tentpole Scene, we will make the middle slog a lot less slogarific, if that's a word.

I will apologize right now and tell you that there are actually *two* different parts to the Midpoint Tentpole: the internal version and the external version. Ideally, your book will have both. They don't have to happen at the same time, but they should both happen near the middle of the book.

(Quick aside: Does it have to be exactly in the middle? No. I write short, snappy thrillers and I like the downhill ride to the finale to be quick, so my Midpoint Tentpole Scene is usually a bit later. However, it is truly amazing how many movies you can fast forward to the exact middle and find yourself smack dab in the Midpoint Tentpole Scene.)

The *internal* Midpoint Tentpole Scene is often called the **Midpoint Mirror** — a term coined by author James Scott Bell in his book *Write Your Novel from the Middle*. The mirror is an apt metaphor because this is the moment when the protagonist looks at themselves and thinks — *What have I become?* Or, *What do I really want?* Or, *I know what's important to me now!* Or, even, *I can't do this!*

What the character sees in the mirror is her **Flaw** (with a capital F). But this flaw won't get fixed until the Choice Tentpole Scene. Up to the Midpoint Tentpole, we the readers have been aware of the flaw, but the protagonist has not. Now, they rip the Band-Aid off and finally see what's holding them back.

I repeat, this is NOT where they fix the flaw. This tension, between knowing the flaw and overcoming the flaw, will help drive the remainder of your second act and make it a lot less soggy, because you'll know your purpose.

Now, the *external* Midpoint Scene: This is sometimes known as the **Raising the Stakes Scene**. This is when the *external* plot kicks it up a notch. Not only can the protagonist not turn back, but the consequences of failure ratchet up.

In *Avengers: Endgame*, the heroes go back in time to collect the Infinity Stones. Not only does it go badly, but it tips off Thanos that something is going on, and he decides to come to Earth to find out what it is. Suddenly the stakes of the movie shift, instead of trying to bring back all of their lost friends, the Avengers now have to stop Thanos from annihilating *everyone*. The stakes have definitely been raised.

Quite often, this will be where the **Ticking Clock** shows up. (Don't you love all these gimmicky names? I know *I* do! I love them so much I put them in **bold** the first time I mention them). Like it sounds, a ticking clock means there is a time limit to the plot. If a problem isn't solved before the clock gets to zero, a disaster will happen. This obviously plays well in heist or disaster stories, but is also incredibly effective in romances and fairy tales (See: *Cinderella*)

If your plot already has a ticking clock component, this is where something happens to either make the clock tick faster, or to make the consequences of failure greater than first thought.

As mentioned, the internal and external Midpoint Tentpole Scenes don't *have* to be the same scene, but when an author pulls that off, it can really be effective: *Oh my god, I'm an utter failure* AND *the world is going to blow up in two hours!!*

Let's review, because this is complicated stuff:

- The **story** is internal and is about how a character changes and overcomes a flaw.

- In the Midpoint Mirror Tentpole Scene, the hero recognizes their internal flaw, but can't yet overcome it.

- The **plot** is external. It's what happens to your character from scene to scene.

- The Raise the Stakes scene is when the plot gets exponentially more difficult.

- The Midpoint Mirror and the Raise the Stakes Scenes are both part of the Midpoint Tentpole.

Hopefully, you can see how these two Midpoint Scenes can take your flagging, soggy middle and give it direction and pep. And it gives you choices. Does your protagonist run away after discovering their flaw, and what does it take to get her back in the game? Or, does your character misinterpret their flaw (I just have to try *harder!*) and cause a bigger catastrophe, leading to the Choice Tentpole Scene, which is when they will *really* understand their flaw (Oh, I have to *rely on other people!*).

Bell, the author of *Write Your Book from the Middle*, thinks you should nail this scene down first, and use it to understand where your character must begin, and where they inevitably have to end. This makes good sense, but I think authors don't always fully understand their character's flaws before they start. However, once you *do* have your Midpoint Tentpole in place, you will be able to go back during revisions and really set up the protagonist's flaw in those opening scenes and show the change in the later scenes. In other words, once you nail your Midpoint Tentpole, you can strengthen your Inciting Incident Tentpole and your Choice and Finale Tentpoles.

Tentpole Four: The Choice

This is it! The moment your readers have been waiting for. If, as I said above, a story tells the reader about a character facing a problem they can't avoid, then this is where it has all been leading. The Inciting Incident has upset the protagonist's world. Because of a flaw in her character, she has been unable to deal with that problem, and as a result things have gotten more and more complicated, until finally she reaches the breaking point. She will have to make a choice, and that choice will determine whether she solves the problem and wins the day, or is defeated.

> Every day ... Life Before
> One day... Inciting Incident
> Because of that... Point of No Return
> Because of that... Midpoint Mirror/Raising Stakes
> Until finally... Choice and Finale

Notes about the Choice Tentpole Scene:

- The choice must be hard!

- *The protagonist must make the choice.* The decision can't be made for them.

- The choice must be relate to your protagonist's flaw and the theme of your book.

- The choice must change your protagonist forever.

Let's discuss. How hard does the choice have to be? Hard. Genius editor Shawn Coyne of Story Grid fame describes the two most common choices as the **Best Bad Choice** and the **Irreconcilable Goods**.[iii]

In the Best Bad Choice, guess what? Both choices suck. The hero must do the best with what they have, knowing someone is going to get hurt in the process and that things will never be the same.

With Irreconcilable Goods, the hero can make a choice that is good for themselves or good for others, but not both, and yes, things will never be the same after.

Irreconcilable Goods are about sacrifice, Best Bad Choices are usually about sticking with your values. And hey, did you notice? *Things will never be the same for the protagonist after.*

And while this sounds bad, it sometimes ends up better for the protagonist than they thought possible, and their inner need and outer want are both fulfilled. Or sometimes, the result is bittersweet, and the protagonist gives up their outer want, only to find they have satisfied an inner need. In *The Corrections*, by Jonathan Franzen, three siblings strive mightily for their individual wants, and they all fail spectacularly. Yet, at the end of the book, the reader feels that they have each grown up a bit, and will be better people moving forward, even though they didn't get what they thought they wanted.

And, of course, in a tragedy, the protagonist usually cannot overcome their flaw and ends up dead (See also, *Othello*.).

Tentpole Five: The Finale

Finally! The Finale. It's just what it sounds like. What is going to happen at the end? If you know that before you start, the writing gets easier, even if you decide to change the Finale completely when you get there. Here are two important ideas to keep in mind when writing your Finale Tentpole Scene (or Scenes).

> Make sure it follows the internal logic
> of the world you've built.

It's all been leading up to this, and that's important. This is the scene or sequence of scenes that are a direct consequence of the Choice Tentpole Scene. That choice was made possible by the Midpoint Tentpole Scene, which would never have happened if the Inciting Incident Tentpole Scene hadn't thrown the protagonist's life into turmoil. They'd still be running that little yarn shop their great aunt bequeathed them and would never have solved the murder and saved the town!

These things all need to tie together. Your Finale can't come out of left field and not relate to what's gone before. Even *Monty Python and the Holy Grail* (which ends suddenly when modern day police arrest Arthur and the other knights for the murder of a television historian) had some little bits of foreshadowing.

People are most aware of this need for connection in mysteries and thrillers, where a reader will feel unfulfilled if the clues weren't properly laid. They want to say, "I should have seen that coming, but I didn't!" Mysteries don't work when there is no consistent internal logic.

It's not just for mysteries, though, it's for all genres. If your Finale is directly based on the character arc you have built for your book, it is going to resonate with the reader.

Let me say that again: If you base your Finale on your character's flaw and on the choice they have to make in the Choice Tentpole Scene, your book will hum with energy and logic and *connection* with your protagonist.

For instance, if your character needs to learn to be true to themselves, but they seduce the girl through an elaborate ruse that is never unmasked, your story is going to fall flat. That's why in stories that involve dress-up, like *Tootsie*, or *The Merchant of Venice,* there is always an unmasking at the end. There's an entire sub-genre of romance based on "pretend" lovers who actually fall in love through the course of the novel. You probably understand all this, at a subconscious level, but it's good to keep in mind. Your Finale Tentpole Scene must connect to your character's central story of internal change.

Go Big or Go Home

I run into this a lot reading first-time manuscripts:

The finale has to be bigger, I tell them.

But it doesn't seem realistic, the author responds.

I.   Don't.   Care.

There's a technique that I'm going to introduce in Chapter 9 for making your scenes bigger, but for now, let me just say that what reads as "big" to *you* will not seem as big to your audience. Because, shhhh, *stories aren't real*. And readers are experts. Experts with expectations. Yeah, they are going to call bullshit when you take it over the top (See also: *Fonzie, Shark Jumping*), but they also want you to push that limit as far as you can.

The reader, above all, wants memorable characters that they love. But why do they *love* them? They *like* them for their witty banter. They *like* them for their good hearts. But they *love* them when they can relate to them.

Why do they relate to them? Because they have watched them face hard decisions and fail. Let me amend that: They've watched them face *increasingly difficult* decisions and fail. That's why the decision your protagonist makes in the Choice Tentpole Scene has to be the hardest decision yet, and the Finale Tentpole Scene that follows has to be the biggest emotional payoff you can manage.

There's a moment at the end of *Return of the Jedi*, when the Millennium Falcon bursts out of the flaming Death Star at the last possible second: Lando raises his arms and shouts in amazement; his little co-pilot Nunb does the same thing. When I was thirteen years old and first saw that scene, everyone in the theater, including me, also whooped or shouted "Yes!!" out loud.

That is what you're looking for. Whether it's a space opera or a romance or a cozy mystery. That is how big you want your Finale to be. But hey, no pressure. We'll get you there.

Other Scenes and Genre Conventions

Okay, that was a lot of information, and it only covered five scenes. Aren't you glad I didn't insist on using Blake Snyder's 15 scene Beat Sheet?[iv] Which is excellent, btw, but don't go looking for it now! We're on a mission to keep this simple. There will be many other scenes in your story, of course, but these Five Tentpole Scenes will get you started. We'll talk about other scenes you are going to want to be sure to have, based on your genre, later in the book. But now, we need to get on to our next step.

And our next step is finding your characters.

Chapter 2 Review:

Oooh, so much information. And this is after I've collected it all and streamlined it and slimmed it down. I've really tried to make it logical and minimal, which means I strongly believe everything you've just read in this chapter is important. To highlight:

- Story structure is important when writing your first draft because it will help you when you don't know where to go.

- The structure of your character's internal journey is more important to know than the structure of their external journey (the plot).

- You CAN do this! Don't be overwhelmed!

- The Five Tentpole Scenes are important moments in the journey of your protagonist. If you know them before you start writing, the writing WILL be easier.

- Make big choices. What seems over the top to you will seem fine to your reader.

- You can do this!!

Chapter 3: Creating Your Characters and Finding (or not finding) Your Theme

Character and Plot, the chicken and the egg. Which came first? It depends on you, and that crazy little imagination of yours.

Did you sit across from an unusual person on the subway and think, "That person would make a *great* character in a book?" Or, were you sitting on a subway and suddenly thought, "What if we went into a subway tunnel and came out in a *different dimension?*"

Either way works, and the beauty of inspiration is that you never know where you'll find it. But, once you have it, you need to focus on creating your character arc. Remember, story is about character change. Always.

So, did you come up with the protagonist first? Great. Picture that character in your head. Now, take a blank sheet of paper and jot down some information.

(Or use our handy worksheet at authorhelp.net/character)

What makes this character appealing to you?
Why did you pick them in the first place?

What is this character's external goal?
This doesn't have to be the plot of the story; it has to be what your character *thinks* the plot of their story is. Does that make sense? For instance, in *Gone with the Wind*, Scarlett's initial external goal is to steal Ashley's love, but her goal eventually becomes to survive the war and save her family's land. External goals can change.

What is this character's internal need?

This is usually unknown to the character at the start of the novel. Scarlett O'Hara thinks her strengths are her charm and her ability to get what she wants by manipulating others. She needs to reject her false strengths and learn to rely on herself.

Why is this protagonist the best possible person to complete this goal?

This can encompass both outer skills and inner strengths. Scarlett cares deeply about her home and has a core inner strength that makes her unstoppable when others would give up.

What is the flaw or misbelief that will keep this character from completing their goal? If they don't have one, give them one. Scarlett

O'Hara believes her beauty and cunning can get her whatever she wants.

Why is this protagonist the worst possible person to complete this goal?

Wait, how can they be the best person AND the worst person for the job? Irony, my friend. And it's this irony that will elevate your story to the next level. When you can combine these two opposites in your Choice and Finale, magic will happen. Need an example?

In *The Lord of the Rings*, who is the best possible hope for destroying the Ring? Answer: The one with the purest, least corruptible heart. A hobbit.

Who is the *worst* possible person to complete this goal? A small, humble person who has no adventuring skills and doesn't even where shoes!

In *The Hunger Games,* who is the best possible Tribute? A girl with excellent survival skills, incredible determination, and a strong sense of honor. But, when Katniss gets to the Capitol, it turns out that much of the game depends on currying political favor, sobering up their drunken mentor, and forming a romantic alliance. Katniss is just about the worst possible person for that situation.

We'll work more on this irony when we formulate our Finale Tentpole Scene.

Believe it or not, if you've answered these character questions for your protagonist, you can begin filling in your Five Tentpole Scenes. It's true, and to prove it to you, I'm going to make up a character and a plot, right now, while sitting at my desk. In less than five minutes. Ready? Here we go.

What is my character's flaw or misbelief that will keep them from completing their goal? Since I don't have anything readily in mind, I'm going to randomly open *The Emotional Wound Thesaurus* by Ackerman and Puglisi, and assign my character, Hazel, an **emotional wound** (I've also decided her name is Hazel).

Drumroll, please... *Failing to save someone's life.* Okay, that's a doozy, but I got this: *When Hazel was a student teacher, a boy in her class choked to death on a pencil eraser.*

What flaws or misbeliefs might this build into Hazel's character? For a misbelief, we can match it up with this: *Hazel believes the child's death was her fault, and she could have prevented it if she had been more prepared.* This could lead to many flaws, but let's go with: *Controlling.* Hazel wants to keep all the details of any situation under control. That's how you keep people safe. She changed her major to physics and engineering, and now is an industry expert on safe and effective high-speed rail.

What is this character's internal need? Hazel needs to realize that she can't save everyone, and to let go of her guilt.

What is this character's external goal? To make up for her past failure by keeping people safe.

What makes this character appealing to you? Hazel faces fear and does the right thing anyway.

Now, I need to brainstorm a conflict that will make this person the best AND worst person for the situation. Hazel is overseeing a prototype of a new high-speed train. She knows the train better than anybody. There is a classroom of students on the train because they won a contest. The train goes out of control. Hazel is the only one with the knowledge to bring them to safety. The fear of making the wrong choice and seeing kids die paralyzes Hazel.

Okay, pretty generic and straightforward, but I only gave myself five minutes. We'll add irony later. Do I have my Five Tentpole Scenes?

Inciting Incident: A prototype high-speed train goes out of control during its inaugural run

Point of No Return: Hazel, the chief engineer, promises the skeptical authorities and the children that she can fix the problem and stop the train before it reaches Duluth, so they put her in charge.

The Midpoint: *Raise the Stakes:* Hazel's first plan fails when a meddling kid breaks an important piece of equipment, and the train picks up speed instead of slowing down. *Mirror Moment:* The evil chief bureaucrat on the train wrests control of the situation from Hazel and blames her for everyone's imminent death. She absorbs the criticism and abdicates responsibility.

The Choice: Thrust back into control after the sudden demise of the Bureaucrat, Hazel must decide whether to revert to her original, overly controlling plan, or try something new that would include working with the children to fix the brakes. Is she willing to release control, and even embrace a risk to others, for the greater good?

The Finale: In a series of exciting successes and reversals, Hazel and the children successfully stop the train without killing anyone.

Not bad. Did I make it seem easy? I've often heard it said that ideas are easy, it's execution that's difficult.

In case you doubt that this is a reliable, repeatable method, I'm going to do it again. Here we go.

What is my character's flaw or misbelief that will keep them from completing their goal? Since I don't have anything readily in mind, I'm going to randomly open *The Emotional Wound Thesaurus* by Ackerman and Puglisi, and assign my character, Samir, an emotional wound (I've also decided his name is Samir).

Drumroll, please...*Growing up in the shadow of a successful sibling.* Okay, that's quite different from Hazel's story. What to do with it?

Samir, who is 22, grew up an average kid in New York City. His brother Omar, who looks very like him, was discovered by an advertising agency when he was 18 and had his face plastered all over the subways. Last year, Omar parlayed his modeling career into a successful singing career with a number one hit and a breakthrough TikTok video. Samir graduated college early and has been struggling since then to write his first novel. He is constantly mistaken for Omar. The flaw this has led to is self-doubt, which shows itself as *cynicism* and a *sense of injustice.* Because Samir is mistaken for Omar, he feels it is only luck that made Omar famous instead of him, and that life is unfair.

What is this character's internal need? Samir needs to create his own art, and not judge it against his brother or society.

What is this character's external goal? To win the love of Ginni, a young woman at a publishing company.

What makes this character appealing to you? Samir has a real ability to see worth in others.

Now, I need to brainstorm a conflict that will make this person the best AND worst person for the situation. Samir falls in love with the perfect person, because of his ability to see worth in others, but believes Ginni only loves him because she thinks he is Omar.

Inciting Incident: When Samir submits his novel about sibling rivalry to a publishing company, Ginni sees him and thinks he is Omar, submitting under a pseudonym. She confronts him and he asks her out without telling her he is actually Samir.

Point of No Return: Samir allows Ginni to introduce him to her family as Omar without telling her the truth.

The Midpoint: *Raise the Stakes:* When the publishing company accepts his novel, Samir realizes he has to tell Ginni the truth. *Mirror Moment:* Samir can't believe what he's done to Ginni, and he realizes that his book is capitalizing on his relationship with Omar. He rejects the book contract and leaves the city to work for World Central Kitchen in Ukraine.

The Choice: Samir returns to New York for the publication of a series of profiles he did while in Ukraine. Will he find Ginni and apologize?

The Finale: Samir avoids Ginni, who is still mad until she sees the amazing work Samir has done while he's been away. He apologizes, she accepts, and they live happily ever after.

I hope this shows you a few things. One, it's true that ideas are cheap; execution is key. Two, these structural components don't only work in the thriller or adventure genres; the same concepts work for romance and literary fiction as well. The stakes are different, as are the plot points, but the same Five Tentpole concept holds true: Inciting Incident, Point of No Return, The Midpoint, The Choice, The Finale.

If you're the type of person who finds the situation first, you simply turn this entire process on its head. For instance, perhaps one day you are on a train and you think, "What if this were a prototype bullet train, and it suddenly went out of control?" That's a pretty good plot. But the important thing to remember is that it is a *plot,* not a *story.* A story is about how the plot changes the main character. So, your next step would be to create that character, just like we did above.

Visualizing Your Character

Now that you've discovered your main character's deep inner turmoil, it's time to get a little shallower and figure out what they look like. There's two easy ways to do this. You can write a page of description, and keep it handy as you write your book, or, you can cheat.

The best way to cheat is to simply find a picture of a person that is close to how you had imagined your character in your head. This could be a celebrity, it could be a friend or relative, or it can just be an image you found on Google. For instance, in one of my novels, the male lead was based on Benjamin Bratt, and the female lead was a fabulous photo I found by Googling "30-year-old Japanese-American woman." You don't have to worry about copyright, because you won't use the actual image for anything except your own reference. And you don't have to worry about readers "recognizing" an actor you are using, because their personality, voice, and other characteristics will be different.

To keep your characters memorable and distinct, it's useful to give them an unusual physical characteristic. This seems like an easy cheat, and of course it is, but that doesn't mean it doesn't work. Just remember, you're going to be stuck with that characteristic throughout the book, so if you give your character a stammer, you're going to have to be consistent with that throughout all their dialogue. If you give them a wooden leg, it's going to affect how you write chase scenes (not to mention sex scenes). The danger of getting carried away here is obvious, but you can see how effective it can be in something like *The Umbrella Academy* (both a graphic novel and a TV series) to have each member of the family have distinct physical traits.

Character Voice

Can you really call something a rabbit hole if all the information you find is useful? I'm thinking here about dialogue. Over the last few years, I've come to consider dialogue to be the most important aspect of the writing craft. When working correctly, your dialogue conveys emotion, character, theme and plot in a way that feels natural and unlabored to the reader. It's the "show" part of the classic "show don't tell" writing maxim.

What cemented my already high regard for dialogue was my discovery of *The Dialogue Doctor Podcast*. The Dialogue Doctors, Jeff Elkins and Laura Humm, are experts at how people talk to each other. It's their actual day job to create scripts that organizations use to help navigate stressful situations. I encourage you, after you've finished your first draft, to check out The Dialogue Doctor. I predict it will be your greatest single influence on your second draft.

Until then, so that you can actually make it through your first draft, I'm just going tell you briefly about character voice and voice modulation. **Character voice is how your character interacts with other people; voice modulation is how that voice changes when the situation changes.** If you want to avoid your characters all sounding just like you — sometimes known as "mono mouth" — then you need to proactively give them distinctive voices and modulations.

Again, this is mostly second draft stuff, but if you put a little work into character voice before you get started writing, it will give you better results right out of the gate. Not only that, but how character voice will affect your plot choices at the scene level will amaze you. Conflict in a scene will jump off the page when you match up two characters with conflicting voices.

Each of your characters should have a baseline voice. Write a quick description on your character sheet of that baseline voice that lists these four things:

Word choice: What kind of words do they use? Educated, slangy, self-conscious, self-centered?

Cadence: Are they a slow talker? Do their thoughts trail off? Long sentences or short sentences?

Pacing: Do they always talk first, do they interrupt often, or are they hesitant? Cadence is *how* they talk; pacing is *when* they talk.

And finally, **Body Language.** Yes, body language is a big part of dialogue, too. Do they talk with their hands? Do they avoid eye contact? Do they cross their arms defensively?

For your protagonist and your antagonist, jot down notes on their voice for these four categories. It doesn't hurt to do it for your two or three biggest supporting characters as well.

Next, how does that voice modulate? Changing the character's voice in a logical and incremental way as their emotional situation changes will make them seem very real.

For each major character, write this sentence three times:

When this character is _____ **(emotional state),**
they _____ **(modulation).**

What you put in the first blank depends on what kind of book you are writing. In a thriller, you might use *stressed, afraid,* and *angry.* In a romance, you might use *nervous, excited,* and *sad.*

There're dozens of answers to these questions, and your choices should come from what you've invented for your character's backstory.

For instance:

When Bob is angry, he paces and talks more loudly.

When Avram is angry, he shuts down physically and uses shorter responses.

When Elaine is angry, she talks heatedly with long, rambling sentences.

These are three perfectly sensible modulations for anger, depending on the character you want to create. Even if you don't nail this on your first draft, just being aware that characters speak and react differently depending on their emotional state will have a positive effect on your scene work and, like good brushing, will help defeat mono mouth.

On the Authorhelp.net website you will find a free pdf character worksheet.

Antagonist and Side Characters

A good bad guy goes a long way. How much work should you put in to designing the villain and the side characters? For the villain, it would be ideal if you did ALL the same prep work that you did for your protagonist. Give them a flaw, give them internal and external goals, give them a distinctive voice with modulations. The more you can do, the better. A good villain believes they are the hero of the story, so make them act like a hero. Have them pursue their goals because they truly believe it's for the best. Give them a flaw that they are not only going to fail to overcome, but that the protagonist will exploit when the time comes.

For supporting characters, do as much as you feel like, but keep it simple. You're not sure how and when you will use your side characters, so you want to keep them vague. Some side characters you will probably invent on the spot as you're writing. In later drafts, you'll go back and make sure those characters look, act, and sound real and consistent. But for now, keep it simple!

Theme

Wait, why is **Theme** here, in the Character chapter? Because theme is best conveyed by the choices your characters make, not the plot or structure of your book.

I'm going to be honest with you: You might not grasp your theme on your first draft. That's okay! Your focus is to find your character's story and bring it to life through the plot. It can easily happen that you get to the end of your draft without quite knowing what the theme or themes of your novel are. Sometimes, it takes an outside reader to tell you what your book is really about.

On the other hand, some authors *start* their story idea with theme. I *want to write a story about how kindness leads to healing. I want to write a story about love being more important than money. When we work together, we all win. When you believe in yourself, others will believe in you, too.*

"So, Tom, you're saying Theme is just a cliché?"

I am. But it is the cliché that you believe, and the one you want to share, and your unique storytelling will reveal that theme in a way that is anything but cliché.

That's all I'm going to say about theme for the purposes of a first draft. If you've got one, great. Use it to identify the flaws of your characters and unify your story telling. If you don't have one, don't sweat it. That's what the second draft is for.

Bringing it all in line

This has been a big chapter, so let's recap the important takeaways.

- Story is more important than plot. The plot is what happens; the story is how what happens changes your main character.

- The way your main character changes is by confronting a deep flaw, or by seeing through the lie that they have been telling themselves.

- Consciously or unconsciously, that flaw is likely related to a larger theme that you, the author, are interested in discussing.

- The reader will be interested in what you have to say

if you present your story through distinctive, believable characters that the reader can relate to. It's not about your characters being the best, the brightest, or the most honorable. It's about making their struggles *relatable*.

- Your character is relatable when they struggle against a deep flaw that has been holding them back for a long time and, through perseverance, overcome it for the betterment of themselves and others.

In many ways, your character prep work drives your plot on a global level and also on a scene level. You cannot overestimate the importance of character and its influence on every part of your novel.

Now, what's your book about again?

Chapter 4: Logline, Pitch, and Outline

Succinct, informative, catchy. I'd like to tell you that this chapter will be all of those things. I'll try. But what I'm actually talking about is your next step: turning your character work and Tentpole Scenes into Logline, Pitch, and Outline.

"So, what's your book about?"

If you can't answer this question in one sentence, then you aren't ready to write yet. Why? Because you must save yourself from yourself. In your mind, you've created the incredible world of your novel, maybe down to granular detail, but the first step in getting it out of you and onto the page in a manner that will appeal to readers is to *focus*. Your logline and pitch are going to help you focus on the story you want to tell, because — if done right — they describe the plot AND the story. Your outline will be more likely to change as you go, as it has more pure plot points, and it's possible that you'll discover better plot ideas to advance your story as you write. Outlines are flexible, but if you change your logline, you're really writing a different book.

Or worse, your description is so vague that it doesn't give your writing compass a strong magnetic north.

"Well, it's about a police detective, but it's not really a mystery, it's more of an exploration of honor, because the hero, who's a great detective but has a gambling problem, has agreed to do a favor for an old friend, not knowing the old friend is now involved with the mob. Not only is the

detective now mixed up in the mob, but he's fallen for the lover of his old friend, so there's two issues of honor at stake — plus his gambling addiction — it's really a multifaceted look at the inability of even good people to act honorably in today's murky moralism."

You may, in fact, end up with all of these ideas in your novel, and do it in a way that works. Maybe. More than likely, you are going to get lost in the weeds along the way, rewriting, adding, and deleting. You might include entire scenes that don't serve your story except in the most tangential way and muddy your message with too much information. A strong logline and pitch, pasted above your screen or tattooed on your forearm, is an essential guide to staying on track.

Logline

So what, exactly, is a logline? Simply, it's what you put on the movie poster (I *know* you've already imagined the movie adaptation in your head). It's one sentence. The best, strongest loglines are two clauses, with the first clause being about the *plot*, and the second line being about the *story*.

"When a well-meaning attempt to help an old friend pulls him into the world of organized crime, a talented but flawed detective must struggle to find his own morality in a world of gambling, mobsters, and seduction."

Is this better than what I had before? Heck, I sure hope so! Do we know what genre our story is? Yes: crime. Do we have our plot? Yes: the book is about a detective who gets involved with the mob while trying to help an old friend. Do we have our story? Yes: Can a man, already damaged by addiction, find and cling to his own sense of honor in a challenging world?

Can we now expand this to list our Five Tentpole Scenes? Let's try:

Inciting incident: Detective Dieter gets a call from an old friend, Armand, asking for a favor.

Point of no return: Dieter learns that his friend's "favor" involves the mob, but he does it anyway because he is uncontrollably attracted to his friend's new lover, Marlene.

Midpoint: *Raising the Stakes:* His division investigates Detective Dieter for alleged mob involvement. *Mirror Moment:* Dieter has a showdown with his boss *and* his friend and realizes that he has lost his honor and his integrity.

Choice: Dieter can regain his honor by rejecting Marlene and betraying Armand in a sting operation, or he can double cross the cops, the mobsters, and Armand and run away with Marlene and a lot of stolen money.

Finale: After a severe loss at the casino makes Dieter choose the dishonest route, the cops raid the mobsters while Dieter and Armand are there. When Dieter sees good cops killed, he changes sides and helps take down the mobsters, even though he may end up in prison.

These five scenes make a serviceable plot outline for a book with the logline we wrote. But you could write ten different plots that told the same *story*. Get it? I keep coming back to this difference between story and plot because it is so important, both in making sure your book does what you want it to do, and for keeping you focused and on track. The logline is the distillation of the Five Tentpole Scenes, and if you refer to it often, it will help you stay focused and moving forward.

Pitch

Earlier, we talked about the Pixar Pitch. With our logline and our Five Tentpole Scenes, we should be able to create our pitch. It's sometimes called an elevator pitch, because you should be able to tell it to someone in the time it takes to ride an elevator — say, thirty seconds.

You don't have to structure your pitch like a Pixar Pitch, but since they have a pretty good track record, let's do it their way:

"Every day, Police Detective Dieter fights an inner battle between his dedication to his job and his gambling addiction. One day, he agrees to do a favor for his old friend Armand, who turns out to be connected to the mob. Because of that, he falls under suspicion from Internal Affairs, and his life becomes an unbearable series of stresses and secrets until finally, he must choose between a daring betrayal and escape, or come clean to the cops and face the consequences of his actions."

Hmm. Something happened there while crafting that pitch. Because the pitch must be short, it causes you to dial down your focus. Do you see what's missing? It's Marlene. While the logline tries to squeeze the romance in by adding the word "seduction," this pitch doesn't even have that. In focusing the pitch, I had to choose what the key story conflict was going to be. Love or honor? In this case, I chose honor. There might be romance and sex in the plot, but the character's story arc is going to focus on honor.

What if my book is really about love, though? Maybe I'm tossing around a theme like *"Obsession corrupts honor."* That could really work with what I've got sketched out so far. Let's try it:

> "*Every day, Police Detective Dieter fights a punishing inner battle between his dedication to his job and his gambling addiction. One day, he meets Marlene when he agrees to do a favor for his old friend, Armand. Because of that, he becomes infatuated with Marlene and continues helping Armand even when it turns out the 'favor' involves the mob. Because of that, he comes under suspicion of Internal Affairs and his life becomes an unbearable series of stresses and secrets until finally, he must choose between the love and risk that has made him finally feel alive inside, or his honor as a detective.*"

All that's really changed here is motive, right? Dieter is going to do what he's going to do, but this time it's because of his obsession with Marlene and the way it makes him feel, and not about friendship.

Interestingly, my first inclination would be to go with pitch number one and write a good old fashion hard-boiled noir about a man whose personal honor is his code, and therefore the central spine of the story. However, as I wrote the second pitch, I saw a stronger conflict in not only the effect passion can have on character choices, but this idea that committing crime and falling in love has brought something vital to Dieter's sad life that is going to be difficult to let go of when it comes time to choose. Remember, the choice should be as difficult as possible.

While Dieter's story is not a book I'm writing, or intending to write, it is a good hypothetical and makes my point. Your pitch is your north star. Tack it to your wall and look at it every day. When you're fleshing out your outline, use it to decide which scenes you need and which you don't. Or, use it during revisions to help you cut out whatever doesn't move the story forward. When you pause and think, *What would the character do now?* consider your pitch and the central character choice that the novel is built on, and let that be your guide.

If you constantly want to stray from your pitch, you need to step back and make sure you still want to go where your pitch is telling you to go. It's okay to change your pitch. Really, it is. What becomes a problem, though, is when your manuscript and your pitch don't sync up but you keep on floundering ahead. Stop, back up, and rethink your story until the pitch and the outline match.

This is a book for inexperienced authors, and one thing I see with first drafts of first books — over and over — is a difficulty in finding the strong thread of the story. When editing, I often cut a third or more of a first draft, even if the author started with a full outline.

Because you've spent ages, possibly years, thinking about your story, it's hard for you not to include everything you've thought of. But not all of it belongs.

My guiding question is always, "But what do you want the book to really be about?" And if you can't tell me in thirty seconds or fewer, it's hard to help. So, take the time and make that pitch!

Outline

As we get close to actually writing—trust me, we are getting close — you now have to decide what you want to do about an outline. Do you already have one? Great. Dust it off and examine it. Does it fit in with all the things we've been discussing? Can you find the Five Tentpole Scenes? Can you distill it down to a pitch and a logline? If not, you might think about redrafting it. If you can find all those things, hell, what are you even doing here? Go write your book, already.

If you haven't written your outline yet, make a choice now:

1. Don't write one
2. Write one

So simple. Remember, you have already figured out your Five

Tentpole Scenes, so even if you decide not to build out a full outline, you still know where your character is starting, where they are going, and what conflict they will be facing. You can stick to that structure and still have lots of room to improvise as you go.

If you decide to create a full outline, good for you! But be careful. This is another area where you can invest a lot of time in researching methods. Methods for the actual outline, as well as methods for keeping track of it all.

This is going to come as a surprise, but my advice is to not overthink it. Ideally, you want a one sentence description for each scene. Let's call that our **Scene Sentence**.

Let's define a "scene" as one unit of action that takes place in a single space or time. That can differ greatly from a chapter; or you might like brief chapters and have just one scene per chapter.

Every good scene contains a conflict, a choice, and a consequence. If you like cliffhangers, then one scene per chapter doesn't always work, because your chapter breaks might actually be in the middle of a scene, with the consequence coming at the start of the next chapter.

But how do you actually organize your outline? You can go old school and write each scene on an index card and then tape them up on the wall. You can open a Google Doc and create a bullet point for each scene. You can use fancy software. Despite what people might tell you, the method isn't that important.

What is important is knowing that your outline is not only telling you what is happening next, it's also telling you the *pacing* of your story. Your outline will have an Inciting Incident, a Point of No Return, a Midpoint, a Choice, and a Finale. Lay them out.

Now, I know you've been thinking about your book for a long time. You've probably got a bunch of scenes already in mind. Add them in between the Five Tentpole Scenes, remembering to keep to one sentence per event: *Bob meets Arlo*, or *Meteor strikes Earth*.

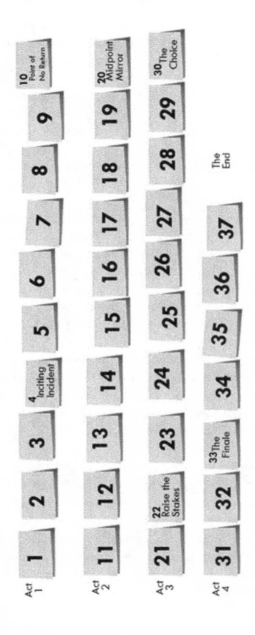

Now step back and look at the balance of your outline. How many bullet points/index cards do you have between Scene One and the Inciting Incident Tentpole Scene? Twelve? That's too many! How many between the Inciting Incident and the Point of No Return? Etc., etc.

It should be easy to tell if your outline is out of balance. If it takes ten scenes before you get to the Point of No Return, and your outline only has twenty scenes, your readers are going to be waiting too long for the plot to kick in. If your Midpoint is actually at the 75% mark, your Finale is going to be rushed and you probably won't have time for the character work you want to do.

This process should result with you adding scenes, or at least adding place markers for scenes you intend to add. And, it might cause you to cut scenes, in which case you must rely on your pitch and logline to be sure you are keeping your focus tight.

You can be loose with this, with lots of blank scenes waiting to be discovered, or you can be super specific. Many screenwriters know exactly how many index cards they want in each act, and where maybe 15 specific types of scenes will show up out of their 30 total scenes. Novels give you a bit more room to play around, but you should still have your Five Tentpole Scenes and you should properly space them to hold up your story (*That's why I call them Tentpole Scenes!! Get it??*).

Want to take it to the next level? Here's a simple exercise:

Read your first Scene Sentence. Now say, "Because of that," and then read your second Scene Sentence. Now say, "Because of that," and then read your third, and so on. Does it work? Do the actions of one scene cause the actions of the next? If they do, you've got a nice tight outline to start with.

Here's the first eight scenes for our novel about Dieter the Smitten Gambling Detective:

1.   Dieter has a hard shift at work and is stressed out and dressed down by his boss. Because of that...

2.   He goes to his favorite casino to blow off steam and stays too long because he is an addict. Because of that...

3.   He misses his arranged appointment at a coffee shop with his childhood friend Armand. Because of that...

4.   He visits Armand at the club where he works and meets and flirts with Marlene before realizing she is Armand's lover. Because of that...

5.   He is already smitten before he realizes his mistake, and he hangs around the club even after he realizes that Armand's involved with the mob. Because of that...

6.   Another detective sees him as he is leaving the club at the same time as a known mob hitman, Jimmy Knuckles. Because of that...

7.   Internal affairs questions Dieter. Spooked, he arranges to meet Armand to tell him he can't help, but instead Marlene shows up to the meeting. Because of that...

8.   Etc., etc, etc

You can see our Inciting Incident Tentpole in Scene 4, and our Point of No Return Tentpole in Scene 8. Hopefully, our Midpoint Tentpole will show up somewhere around Scene 20.

Obviously, novels with multiple storylines will have multiple "Because" lines, and some effects of one scene may not be felt until much later in the book. Try to make each scene necessary to the scene that follows it, and if it's not necessary, ask yourself if it really needs to be there.

Okay, enough about outlines.

1 Dieter has a hard shift at work, and is stressed out and dressed down by his boss. Because of that...

5 He is smitten and he hangs around the club even after he realizes that Armand's involved with the mob. Because of that...

2 He goes to his favorite casino to blow off steam, and stays too long because he is an addict. Because of that...

6 He is seen by another detective as he is leaving the club at the same time as a known mob hitman, Jimmy Knuckles. Because of that...

3 He misses his arranged appointment at a coffee shop with his childhood friend Armand. Because of that...

7 Internal affairs questions Dieter. Spooked, he arranges to meet Armand to tell him he can't help, but instead Marlene shows up to the meeting. Because of that...

Inciting Incident!!!

4 He visits Armand at the club where he works and meets and flirts with Marlene before realizing she is Armand's lover. Because of that...

Point of No Return

8 Dieter decides to fall for Marlene's seduction and become involved in the favor, even though he knows he's putting himself in danger.

45

Tie Your Shoes, Gird Your Loins, Sharpen Your Pencils: Time to Start.

Finally, the moment you've been waiting for — writing the goram book. Are you ready? To review, here's what you should have accomplished through Part One of this book. You can skip these things, but it will cost you more time in the long run, and more tears.

1. You've created a protagonist, antagonist, and several side characters.

2. You've created character sheets for them that describe their wants, needs, and flaws.

3. You know what your characters look like.

4. You know what your characters sound like normally, and what they sound like when experiencing certain emotions.

5. You've at least thought about your theme.

6. You've identified your Five Tentpole Scenes.

7. You've crafted a logline and a pitch.

8. You have some kind of outline, ranging from just the Tentpole Scenes with blank placeholders in between to a complete scene by scene progression, one sentence per scene.

Okay, ready? Let's go!

Part Two:
Writing Your First Draft

Interlude: Mindset and Mechanics

This book is largely about character and story, but I wanted to add a brief aside here about mindset and mechanics. As with everything, there are hundreds of opinions on how to get the daily writing done, and what tools to use to do it. I'm going to tell you the ones that I think are the simplest and most effective. Use them or find what works for you. YMMV.

Writing Space: Office, coffee shop, bed, couch. Everyone has an opinion. Less important than where you are is what's around you. Personally, I think the people who say they thrive on white noise are the same people who tell you they are great at multitasking. I don't believe them. It's also been shown that listening to music while doing creative work does not help, even if the music is instrumental. Many, many people will shout me down on this, but I maintain: find a quiet space far away from your usual distractions. I know some people who work on a separate computer that they only use for writing, because it helps train their mind that time spent on that machine is "Writing Time."

Word/Google/Scrivener/Atticus/Etc.: Use the writing program that is easiest for you, and the least distracting for you. For me, that's Google Docs because I can use it from anywhere, and when I'm drafting I don't care that much about formatting. I just keep plowing ahead. Many people are going to make strong, heartfelt recommendations. Keep those recommendations in mind for later. For your first draft, *use whatever you already know how to use.* It will save you time and energy, and keep you focused on writing your story.

Writing sprints: Also called Pomodoro sprints. Set a timer for 20-30 minutes depending on what works for you and do nothing but write words during that time. When the timer goes off, get up, stretch, get a drink of water, think about what you are going to write next. Don't get on social media or make a phone call. Sit down, reset the timer, and go again. This may feel counter-intuitive; if you are in the flow, why would you want to stop? Maybe you won't, but for me and for many people, being in the "zone" wanes after about, well, 20-30 minutes, and if you're really in the zone, taking a five-minute break won't pop you out of it, as long as you aren't shifting your focus to another subject during your break.

Ergonomics: When it comes to posture and such, remember, I'm not a doctor! Make sure you are comfortable. If something hurts, adjust. Most importantly, move around every half hour or so. If you've been sitting, try standing, and vice versa. Don't stay in the same position for too long.

Deep Work: There's a famous book by Cal Newport called *Deep Work*, and all the research I've done on attention and focus confirm and corroborate what Newport recommends: No distractions, no multitasking, and a dedicated amount of time between two and four hours.

For every fan of deep work, there's an author who wrote their book on their iPhone in five-minute spurts while waiting at traffic lights. Fine, but I'm a fan of deep work. For one reason, it fits well with the idea of Pomodoro sprints. A great work session of four thirty-minute sprints with three ten-minute breaks would be two hours a day. Interestingly, studies show that it's hard to keep up creative energy for more than four hours in a row, even if you had more available time in the day (and who has?).

Building a chain: If you can get to the page every day, without missing a day, you begin to build a chain of days. This can be a visible chain if you keep a streak tracker app on your phone or a calendar on your wall. The longer you make the chain, the more obsessed you become with keeping it going. If you break the chain, you might find yourself suddenly missing several days in a row. This is bad for mindset, and also for efficiency because it requires rereading what you already have down to figure out what the heck you were doing when you stopped.

This happens to me a lot. I have a day job, I have kids. I got Covid. I went on vacation. It was Christmas. You name it. Each time I break the chain, I have trouble getting it going again, and as a result I've had times when I put down a project for a few *months*!! Not because of writer's block, but because breaking my chain allowed Resistance creep in, and Resistance feeds on itself until it is much easier to just not do the thing instead of doing it.

How do you beat Resistance?[v] For me, I just need to force myself to get at least one sentence down each day. I just tell myself: "Enough, I'm going to get something down." After a day or two, I find I'm racing past that one sentence and writing as much as I can until it's time to drive a kid to school or wherever the hell I'm supposed to be taking them.

Resistance is weird because you're excited to write this book, right? But you're also scared. Resistance is the secret part of you that is afraid of being judged. It's sneaky and it's going to do its best to derail your first draft.

But you've got this. You've done all the prep work; you've removed the distractions. You've got a story you want to tell, so let's start telling it.

Chapter 5: The First Tentpole — The Inciting Incident

It's time! Hopefully, the first half of this book has put so many ideas in your head that you can't wait to get started. In this chapter, I'm going to guide you from the first page to the first Tentpole Scene. If, in two hours a day, you can manage 500 words per day, you'll get there in about 10 days. Obviously, you may sit down and pour it all out in one marvelous session; or each day might be only 250 words. It can be hard. Just be sure you write something, every day, no matter how little. Start building that chain!

Your opening chapters will introduce your protagonist, set up the world of your story, and give the reader a feel of the tone and style of your writing. But remember, this is a first draft. Don't worry about it being perfect. As you write, your view of the story may darken, and on the second draft you may have to change the tone of the early chapters later. Or vice versa. Despite all the planning we've done, it's very possible for a story to take on a life of its own. That can be a good thing. That's the feeling that Pansters — I mean Discovery Writers — thrill to. It can also mean a lot of revision, but that's for later.

As much as I want you to make your draft quick and impulsive, let's take a moment here to talk about the anatomy of a scene, for the purpose of making your draft both quick and *useful*.

Scenes

I define a scene as a sequence of events that occur in a single time and place. If you think of a play or a movie, it's pretty obvious. In a play, they most often kill the lights between scenes so they can physically set up the new one. In a movie, the camera may cut between characters often within a scene but will usually have a slightly longer transition to a new scene, with a blackout or some kind of fade.

As I've mentioned, a chapter may have more than one scene in it, or a scene may overlap from the end of one chapter to the beginning of another. While drafting, worry about the scene and not the chapter; you can nail down chapter breaks later.

But a scene is more than just a "sequence of events." It is a *specific* sequence of events. This sequence has many names, but if you look at it closely, you'll realize that it's just a smaller version of three of our Tentpoles: Inciting Incident, Choice, Finale. For scene work, and to keep you from getting confused, we're going to call them **Conflict, Choice, and Consequence**[vi] when working on a scene.

Conflict, Choice, Consequence. In every scene. If you don't have these in your scene, you're missing something. So, what are they?

Conflict: Something has to happen in the scene, and it has to upset what was supposed to happen or what a character hoped would happen. It's, you know, a *conflict* (If this were rocket science, I would not be your teacher.). Sometimes it's a conflict with another character, or sometimes a conflict between the protagonist and their situation, or even their emotions. Or sometimes it's something really simple.

For example: *Melva breaks the zipper on her favorite skirt while getting ready for her date with Joy.*

Choice: Your protagonist must make a choice about this

conflict. Face it, avoid it, put it off until tomorrow. And it must be your protagonist that makes the choice. I'll be reminding you of this a lot as we go on, because one of the easiest ways to make sure your story has legs is to make sure your protagonist has *agency*. Don't write a book where lots of things happen *to* the protagonist, write a book where lots of things happen to the protagonist *as a direct result* of the choices they are making! As mentioned in Chapter 2, make the choice as difficult as you can, even if that choice is about something mundane, like which skirt to wear on a date.

Melva breaks the zipper on her favorite skirt while getting ready for her date with Joy. She must choose between the two other skirts in her closet: one is too dowdy and the other is too sexy. Which impression does she want Joy to have of her?

In this example, Thanos isn't killing half the Universe, but for Melva (who hasn't been on a decent date in a long, long time), the stakes are still high.

Consequence: What is the result of the choice? How does it change the trajectory of the story? What does it tell us about our characters? Does it set up the "Because of that" we are looking for to propel us into the next scene? Every scene should either advance plot or reveal character, otherwise it's wasting the reader's time.

Melva wears the sexy skirt and spends the whole date tugging distractedly on it because she is self-conscious. As a result, she doesn't pay enough attention to what Joy is saying and they don't connect on a deeper level. Because of that, Joy rejects an invitation for a second date and Melva becomes even more depressed and lonely.

Poor Melva. She deserves to be happy. Here's an alternative:

Melva wears the sexy skirt and Joy compliments her on it. They have a great night out dancing. Melva has never felt so free, or brave. Because of that, she invites Joy to come home with her and read her manuscript, something she's never let anyone else do.

And here's a third version, just for fun:

Melva wears the sexy skirt and gets a strong response from Joy. They end up in bed, which Melva never does on a first date. Because of that, they have an incredibly awkward breakfast the next morning.

What I'm trying to show you here is that every scene matters. Because the consequence of the scene is going to affect what happens next, each scene will — and should — have a real impact on your global story.

Let me say it again, every scene should advance the plot or reveal character. A great scene will do both.

What Kind of Content, and How Much?

Yes, I hear you. It's all very well to understand the structure, but what, actually, are you writing about in these first few chapters?

The answer to this question can depend a lot on genre, and on your own personal style. A murder mystery could start with a death, or it could start with the detective. A romance could start with a bad break-up, or the first class of the fall semester. An epic fantasy could start with an important proclamation from the king.

Regardless of the genre, the first few scenes are usually going to do the following things (in no particular order):

1. Introduce the setting: Where in the world are we?

2. Introduce the status quo: What's normal around here?

3. Introduce the protagonist: Who is this person and *why should I empathize with them?*

4. Introduce a problem: What keeps the protagonist's life from being ideal?

5. Hit us with the Inciting Incident: Boom!

Notice that I have included both a problem *and* an Inciting Incident. They are not the same thing. The Inciting Incident will be the thing that makes the problem untenable. If we think back to poor old Detective Dieter, his performance at work, exacerbated by his gambling, is his problem. But that's his every day problem (a la Pixar). It's his meeting with Armand and/or Marlene that will *actually* kick off the conflict of the story. The status quo world doesn't have to be perfect. In fact, it shouldn't be.

What the opening scenes of your first draft usually *shouldn't* have:

1. Too much world building — don't dump it on the reader all up front!

2. Too much boring stuff — you want the status quo, but not the status snorefest!

3. A brilliant first line — that's for later drafts. You will be tempted to rewrite the beginning over and over, but that's for later.

4. Every character in the book - you need space and time to introduce your characters.

How many scenes does it take to get from page one to the Inciting Incident? Will you throw the book across the room if I say "It depends"?

Okay, I won't say that then. **Plan for four to six scenes, each between 1,000 and 2,000 words.**

Now, write your first scene. You can do it. I believe in you!

And... cue the crickets.

Still not sure how to start? If you are stuck, try writing your Inciting Incident scene first. It's okay to work on scenes out of order if it helps you get into the groove, and most first-time novelists have been thinking about their Inciting Incident for a long time. It's generally part of their earliest brainstorming. *What would you do if an asteroid was going to hit Earth tomorrow?* Or, *What would you do if you woke up one morning and your child, and every trace of them, was gone?*

If one of those ideas was your premise, you could write a scene where the protagonist is in a traffic jam on the way to work, on the other side of town from her husband and family, and the radio is interrupted with the news of the asteroid. Or, in the second case, you could write a scene where the protagonist bangs open the bedroom door to find that not only is his teenage son gone, but the room has been stripped of everything.

Now go back to page one and think about how to get to that first Inciting Incident.

A woman and her husband quarrel over breakfast because she is spending too much time at work. On the way out the door, she sees that the lawn furniture has been left out overnight even though it is her teenager's job to bring it in. She goes back inside to reprimand them, making herself late to work. On her way to work, she talks on the phone to an old friend about how unhappy she is at home, but her friend is too busy telling her about her own problems and isn't really listening. Then she gets pulled over for failing to signal! While she is gripping the wheel in disgust, the police officer suddenly stops talking to her and grabs the radio from his belt, gripping it to his ear. Abruptly, he turns and gets back in his cruiser and races off. The woman is confused until, as she pulls back into traffic, the song on her radio is interrupted with a special government broadcast about an asteroid.

Or, in the second example:

A woman and her husband quarrel over breakfast because she is spending too much time at work. On the way out the door she sees that the lawn furniture has been left out overnight even though it is her teenager's job to bring it in. She goes back inside to reprimand them, but her sister calls her. She is trying to have a heart to heart, but her husband keeps interrupting. She hangs up the phone intending to kill him but realizes the time and that their teenager isn't up and getting ready for school. She opens the teenager's bedroom door to find that not only are they gone, but so is everything in their room!

In both these cases, the protagonist's problem is the same: she is unappreciated and disconnected from her family. The Inciting Incident is different — Asteroid vs. Alien Abduction — but in either case, it's likely that the Midpoint will involve the woman deciding to no longer blame everyone around her for her failures, and the Choice and Finale will involve saving and reuniting with her family. And hopefully somewhere in there her husband will wise up as well. Jerk.

Can you start the *first* scene of your book with the Inciting Incident? Yes, sometimes you can. One way is to bring it forward to kick off some excitement right on page one. This can work in mystery novels, where the murder is shown in the opening scene, and then the next scene introduces the detective and relates their actions, setting up the status quo for the protagonist. It can work in a zombie novel that starts *after* the catastrophe instead of before.

One of the most outstanding examples of messing with the Inciting Incident is the first episode of the show *Fleabag*, where the inciting incident isn't revealed until the end of the episode, leaving you to wonder for the entire run time what is wrong with the protagonist. But these are really just examples of rearranging the narrative order of the book for tension, and you have to be careful not to shortchange the introduction of your protagonist.

Never forget, story is about character and conflict. While it's important to have conflict in every scene, it doesn't have to be THE major conflict of the book. Instead, it should be a conflict that helps us—immediately—relate to the protagonist.

There's fantastic writing on this topic by Matt Bird in his book, *The Secrets of Story*, but you're not going to go read that book right now, because you are too busy drafting your first novel! Right?

Suffice to say, it's not the physical description, or the moral fortitude of a character, that makes us relate to them. It's identification and connection on some emotional, empathetic level. Otherwise, only readers who are superheroes would relate to stories about superheroes, and only readers who are from Sri Lanka would relate to stories about Sri Lankans. And we know that's not true about fiction.

Life is full of emotional journeys and choices, and our brain uses story to test ride various ways of dealing with these choices without the actual danger of doing it in real life.[vii] Fiction is an empathy machine.

But wait, haven't you been told that the protagonist needs to do something virtuous right at the beginning to make the audience like them? Doesn't she have to "Save the Cat"?

No. That's a misconception. What the protagonist has to do is make a hard choice that the reader can relate to, or suffer a setback that hits home for the reader as well. If that hard choice results in doing something virtuous, then yes, go ahead, save that cat, but only after the conflict in the scene makes saving the cat important to the character.

Let me give some more grounded examples:

- A character who starts the opening scene thinking they are getting a promotion, but instead gets fired

- A person who starts the scene late for their kid's baseball game because they chose to finish the big project for the boss before leaving work

- A person who needs to get to the bank before it closes, but instead climbs a tree to save a cat and then can't make the deposit

- A person who takes special care to make breakfast for their spouse, only to be accused of buttering them up for something

As you can see, some of these are big, some of them are small. Some are part of the conflict of the scene, others are things that happen to the character and elicit an emotional response. By and large, we empathize strongly with characters who are misunderstood, because we ALL feel misunderstood.[viii] Seeing a character want something, but not be able to get it, makes us empathize with them, and as that disappointment repeats throughout the novel, our empathy increases until we finally get a successful payoff in the Finale of the global story.

This first act of the book is when you want to include those scenes that will bind your reader to your protagonist, so that they will follow them anywhere.

Incite the Heck Out of That Incident!

And finally: Go big or go home. You've introduced your protagonist and what ails them, now you are going to introduce the change that is going to rock their world. Don't use half measures. Be sure the world shakes, the palms sweat, the gobs are smacked. If you are inclined to scale things back for the sake of "realism," don't. Most readers are up for a much wilder ride than you think they are. They don't want real life; they want a good story. You can always dial it back in the editing phase.

Reviewing Chapter 5:

Did you make it? If I peek over your shoulder right now, what's your word count? Is it 6,000 to 12,000 words? Is your character and your setting alive on the page? Mostly alive?

Congratulations, I knew you could do it!

Now, I'm going to ask you to do something difficult. DON'T REWRITE ANYTHING YET! People who begin to rewrite their draft after a few chapters will still be rewriting chapter five in eight weeks and will never move on to chapter six. But you will!

Are you not quite there yet? Does the project seem too big? Are all your ideas lame? Are you only getting a few words down per day, or skipping some days completely?

Don't give up!

Instead, take a breath, take a step back, take another breath.

Let's review this chapter:

- You have your Inciting Incident — this is the idea you

thought up oh so long ago, when this novel was just a glimmer in your eye.

- You've figured out where to start by backing up from your Inciting Incident.

- You've got to get from that starting point to that Inciting Incident.

- What's the problem in your character's daily life that is bothering them? Show it in a scene.

- Why should the reader care about your character? Show it in a scene.

- Find a "Because of that..." scene. How does your character's problem make them behave around friends, at work, at home? Show that consequence in a scene.

- How was life better for the character before they had this problem? How do they wish things were? Illustrate that.

Now, take a deep breath, take another one, and try again.

Better this time?

Congratulations. You're on your way!

Chapter 6: The Second Tentpole— Point of No Return

You did it! You got words on the page! I hope you found that the effort you put in at the beginning of this book to find your character and their internal conflict helped when it came to writing your opening scenes.

This chapter is going to cover the next stage of your book, from the Inciting Incident Tentpole Scene to the Point of No Return Tentpole Scene.

First, I want to talk a bit about three-act structure. I've mentioned "Acts" previously but not really explained them. If you've ever seen a play, you've seen acts. Most modern plays are in three acts, Shakespeare was generally five acts, a collection of short skits might be referred to as "An Evening of One-Act Plays."

An act is a collection of scenes that hang together to form one major movement of your story. Therefore, a three-act story will have three major movements. Mostly in today's entertainment world, we see a three-act structure, though some people insist on a four-act structure, which breaks the long middle act in half at the Midpoint Tentpole.

I like three acts, because as you may have noticed by now, three is the magic number. Conflict, Choice, Consequence. Beginning, Middle, End. The Three Story Method, created by J. Thorn and Zach Bohannon, focuses on this trio because it has always been the basis of storytelling, all the way back to Aristotle, one of the earliest drama critics, and back before him probably to cave dwellers telling stories around a fire. A story has a beginning, a middle, and an end, and as a reader we are used to certain things happening in those three acts. If they don't happen it doesn't feel right, so if you are going to mess with the three-act structure you need to be a genius who can get away with it, or you need to be prepared to have some disappointed readers.

We expect a beginning: A conflict that upsets our protagonist's world. We expect a middle: Protagonist struggles mightily to solve conflict. We expect an ending: The conflict rises to a crisis point at the climax of the story and then resolves to some kind of new status quo— the consequence.

Act One of a story, therefore, is generally the first twenty-five percent of the book, and takes the reader from page one to the Point of No Return, the point when the character commits fully to whatever journey awaits them.

When you are reading a book, the author will sometimes actually divide the book into parts. The end of Act One usually being the end of Part One. When you are watching a film, you can almost always *feel* the moment the story moves from Act One to Act Two, so strongly that it's often called the act break, or the Break into Two moment.[ix]

Star Wars is an easy one. (Okay, Star Wars is *always* an easy one because it follows the traditional Hero's Journey so closely). The Inciting Incident is Princess Leia's message to Obi Wan, but the Point of No Return moment is when Luke's family is killed (oops, spoiler), and he decides to go with Obi Wan. His family is gone, his house is gone, and he's choosing to literally leave the planet.

What Happens Now?

So, you say, tapping your foot nervously. *How do I get from the Inciting Incident to the Point of No Return?*

You get there with four to six more awesome scenes. These scenes are going to deepen the reader's connection with the protagonist, introduce some new players and problems, and offer a choice to the hero that is irreconcilable — once made, there is no turning back!

B Story

One thing to think about at this point: Are you going to have a B story, and what it's going to be? A B Story is a secondary plot. It can be another issue that your protagonist has to deal with, or it can be another character's storyline in which your protagonist plays an important role. The B Story might be introduced before the Inciting Incident, or it might not. You might not have a B Story at all if it doesn't fit your purpose.

A useful thing a B Story can do is to help you deepen your protagonist by showing more sides of them. In an action movie, like a disaster thriller, family will often be the subject of the B Story. When a movie-goer watches James Bond beat the bad guys repeatedly, it doesn't do much to bind us closer to Mr. Bond. It can be repetitive, even when we enjoy the action scenes. There's no B Story in a Bond movie. It's all Bond all the time.

Consider instead something like this: A man, Orson, is struggling to get home to his family after an earthquake has shut down the city. His son has a medical condition that requires constant electricity for medical equipment to properly function. The power is out and might be for a long time. Orson needs to get home. He has joined a small group of people doing the same thing, and they work from obstacle to obstacle as they cross the ruined city.

What's a good B Story? One might be a story of family strife, told in flashbacks. The protagonist's single-minded need to provide for the family may have affected his ability to emotionally engage with them. Getting home becomes even more important, because he needs a chance to fix the rift he's caused before everybody is dead.

Another good B Story might involve Fatima, a nurse who saves Orson when the earthquake first hits. Not long after their journey begins, Fatima sees a bus filled with wounded people and insists Orson helps. He refuses, because his priority is his family, so Fatima goes her separate way. What happens to her and how she and the protagonist cross paths again — and what that means about the protagonist — might be a great B Story.

Character Flaw

As you may have guessed from my examples, a good B Story that really deepens a character is going to be connected to the character's main flaw, and that flaw is often already on display as part of the "problem" your character is facing before the Inciting Incident takes place.

Having more than one plot line for the protagonist's flaw helps illustrate and deepen the flaw, which will make the moment the protagonist triumphs even more rewarding to the reader.

To that end, this section of your novel is the perfect time to trot out the character's flaws and misbeliefs. The Inciting Incident has happened, but the protagonist hasn't quite reached the Point of No Return Tentpole Scene. What do you think might be some excellent scenes for this section?

Scenes to Include

Initial reaction to Inciting Incident: Something unexpected and extraordinary has happened. What does your protagonist do? Does she ignore it, and if so, what does that say about her? Does she immediately try to fix the problem and fail, and what does that say about the journey she will need to take? Does she seek advice from a mentor, and where does that advice lead?

The reader needs to see the flaw in the character, the lie that they believe. While the Inciting Incident upends the world of the protagonist, it doesn't yet change the tools and methods she uses to try to fix or take advantage of the problem. Sometimes there isn't even an attempt to fix the problem, just denial — a straight up refusal to face the call to action.

In that case, you are going to want a scene that shows some hard consequences for the choice of inaction. In the four to six scenes after the Inciting Incident, the character must move toward a point where they commit to whatever the main spine of the story is going to be: their External Goal.

External Goal: This is what the character wants, and what they think they need. Through the course of the story, the hero will realize that what they really need — their **Internal Goal** — is something else entirely. The External Goal can change as the plot goes along, and often will. First, Orson will want to get home to his family, but later he will find out that the earthquake was man-made, and he must stop the villain from destroying the entire planet. Something like that.

A Villain: Speaking of villains, we need them to show up now too, or at least our level one villain. Your story may have multiple villains of varying villainy. Readers are hungry for stories of conflict, that's what keeps them hooked, so they are intuitively keeping an eye out for the antagonist as they sink into your story and will be unsettled if they can't find them. They may not consciously *realize* that's what is happening; more likely, they will just get bored and "not really feel" the story.

Your early antagonist doesn't need to be the overall archenemy of your novel, though of course it can be. It just needs to be the person who's standing in the way of your protagonist achieving their current External Goal. And I use the word "person" with intent. Your reader will engage much more with a person than a thing. Is Orson's antagonist the earthquake? Sure, but if you want your scenes to pop, add a *person* to those scenes who has a completely different idea of how to get from one side of the city to the other and interrupts and delays Orson repeatedly. Human villains not only bring connection, but they bring nuance and the opportunity for more dialogue, and dialogue is the best way to convey emotion to your reader.

In these early scenes of your book, the External Goal should be obvious, and it should be just out of reach of your hero. The only way they are going to get it is to jump in, all the way, with no turning back. Half measures haven't worked. Remember, this is the same regardless of genre: It can be embarking on a quest, joining a secret spy society, or asking the new boy out on a date in front of other friends.

Make sure your protagonist is initiating the action.

Protagonist as First Actor: An easy error at the beginning of the book is to have your protagonist be too reactive. It's a common mistake because the Inciting Incident is something that happens, and the protagonist reacts to it. It's easy from there to keep creating reactive scenes, and you want to avoid that.

Readers need to connect with your protagonist. It's the number one thing that will keep them reading. On an intuitive level, readers form deeper bonds with characters that are active and making decisions. As I've said before, they also connect with protagonists that they can empathize with, and when the protagonist has an emotional scene that the reader relates to, empathy is formed. Some of the most intensely empathetic scenarios are: rejection, failure, false accusation, and relief.

So, look for scenes in which your character decides to take action—and it all goes wrong. As a result, someone falsely accuses them of something, they lose something or someone they value highly, or they face off against an antagonist and fail unexpectedly. Then, to keep your reader on an emotional rollercoaster, mix in a scene where the character thinks they are going to fail, but somehow, they grasp victory from the jaws of defeat.

The Point of No Return

Let's talk about the actual Point of No Return Tentpole Scene itself. By this point, you should be eight to twelve scenes into your story. The reader should know the protagonist and their flaws, and the protagonist should have some idea what they are up against. What they don't know, at this point, is how much worse things are going to get, or how wrong they are about what they think is happening. Nevertheless, they are going to step up and make a decision that firmly takes them from Act One into Act Two.

What are some reasons they would make that decision?

False confidence: Your protagonist has had setbacks and successes but chooses to focus only on their successes. They are willfully blind to their flaw and think the path forward will be easy.

Misplaced trust: A mentor or trusted person tells your hero that they are the only one who can save the day, or that there is only one successful path forward.

Clear-eyed commitment: The way forward looks bleak, maybe impossible. Everything has gone wrong, and no one but your protagonist is available to save the day. They know it might not work, but they are going to try anyway.

The quest: The protagonist believes that there is a definite solution out there to the problem and makes it their external goal to find that solution and use it to save the day.

Lost community: Your protagonist has lost all they know and love, so they choose to enter a new world, start on a new quest, because everything they know is gone.

Unique opportunity: Life only happens once, and sometimes you just have to go for it, especially when romance is involved.

These are some ideas for how and why your protagonist might participate in the Point of No Return, but what will the scene be?

Time to look at your character sheet. What is the lie your character believes? What is her deep flaw? What is it you like most about the character? All these questions you answered earlier are now going to help you choose the best plot point for that character.

In the plot we created for Hazel, the engineer, Hazel's flaw is an overwhelming need for control. She also believes a lie: that she is responsible for a child's death. When a bullet train malfunctions and goes out of control, Hazel steps up to take charge.

The scenes between the train going out of control (Inciting Incident) and the Point of No Return (Hazel taking charge), like the scenes *you* are going to write next, would likely include the introduction of a villain (a pompous bureaucrat), refusal to be involved, perhaps a failed attempt at an easy solution, and finally the agreement to take responsibility.

Please note that, as in this case, the Point of No Return element can be psychological or emotional; it doesn't have to be physical. Sometimes it's all three at once (Take the blue pill, Neo!).

For Hazel, she has kept her life private and close, with a firm grip on her self-control. Psychologically, opening herself back up to failure and criticism is a big step that is going to be hard to take back. Thus, it's a Point of No Return moment for her.

Also note that taking this step does not solve Hazel's flaw. Not at all. In fact, her attempts to fix the problem using her old, familiar set of skills is going to exacerbate the flaw, and make things worse, until she faces herself at the Midpoint.

And a last consideration: Think about what comes next. We will talk about it in the next chapter, but the Second Act starts with what I like to call the Promise of the Premise (Stolen from Blake Snyder). It's a series of escalating complications that revolve around the logline of your story. Remember the logline? If you promised your readers a teenager gaining superpowers, these will be the scenes of Peter Parker falling off buildings as he learns how to sling webs. The scenes between the Point of No Return Tentpole and the Midpoint will be the scenes you see clips of in the movie trailer: exciting, unique, fun.

Make sure that you end Act One by thrusting your protagonist into a world where these scenes naturally take place.

Are you ready to keep writing? Great.

Have you managed 500 words a day so far? Yes? Fantastic. Try to keep that up for another 10 to 14 days.

Tips:

Draft! Don't let your new awareness of craft elements cause Resistance. Keep plowing ahead even if you know you're writing crap, even if you're not sure what you're doing matches my suggestions, or even if my suggestions are valid. Just keep going!

Because of that: Make sure each scene directly results from the choice and consequence of the one before it.

Dialogue: Include dialogue whenever possible. Readers make a stronger emotional connection through dialogue, and it helps you to "show" a character's traits rather than "tell" them.

Big Step: This should be self-evident but make the Point of No Return a genuine commitment by your hero. If they can just change their mind, the reader won't feel any tension.

Last but not least, look at your Pitch. Remember the story you set out to tell. Now go create scenes that do just that. You can do it!

Chapter 7: The Third Tentpole— The Midpoint

Welcome back! In my mind you, the author, read each of these chapters and then go off and write your scenes while I sit here anxiously waiting for you to return, eager to find out if my advice was helpful.

If all is going well, then you should be about one quarter of the way into your manuscript. Your protagonist and antagonist should be clearly defined, with wants and needs that drive them to make important choices. After a bit of trial and error, your protagonist has made an irrevocable decision that has set them on a new path.

After you read this chapter, you will go and conquer the next part of your novel, up to and including the Midpoint Tentpole Scene, over the next three weeks. To do this, increase your daily word count to 750 words per day. Yes, I know, not everyone can do this, but use it as a guide and set up a schedule that you think you can manage.

750 words per day for 21 days is 15,000 words. That's somewhere between eight and twelve scenes. Of course, if you want to write 2000 words a day, go for it! And if you're writing an epic fantasy, then maybe you're going to have fifteen or twenty scenes in this section. These are just ballpark figures. Your mileage may vary.

The Promise of the Premise

I took the title for this section from Blake Snyder's *Save the Cat* screenwriting book, a book I've mentioned a lot, because it's full of expert advice and provides an interesting way to look at story structure. Of all his quirky titles and ideas, this is the section that really resonates with me and that I want to make sure you understand.

The premise is what you told your reader the book was going to be about. If your logline is, "A man stranded on Mars must overcome his hopelessness and find a way to survive," then the promise of the premise is going to be scenes of the man trying to survive. It seems simple, sure, but it's easy to wander off into the weeds. That's why you have your logline and your pitch taped up over your computer or written on the back of your hand.

The scenes in this section are going to be a series of escalating complications.

What the what?

Escalating, meaning the challenges get progressively bigger. This drives the pacing of your book and keeps the reader from getting bored. If your protagonist goes to work and has an argument with someone in their office, that's a complication. If they go to work the next day and have a similar argument with someone else in their office, that is also a complication, but it's flat.

This might sound obvious to you but trust me: I've worked on dozens and dozens of manuscripts and this is always a problem with inexperienced authors. Why? I think there are three reasons.

One is that authors often draw from real life, without realizing that real life is boring. A second reason is hesitancy to leave things out. Your reader wants you to skip to the good parts, even if it might make more sense in *your* mind to include every step of the journey. And third is that the author is afraid the reader will think the story is unrealistic, and therefore they dial back the drama (psst — this is a mistake).

Therefore, make sure your complications escalate. Your protagonist gets in an argument with a coworker. The next day, it's announced that there has been a theft in the office and a search of the premises finds the missing item in your protagonist's desk! Your hero is fired, and now must explain to his husband what happened.

Complications don't always have to be bad. They are just things that throw your character out of the status quo and present them with a difficult choice. Don't forget about choice! When we deal with conflict, choice, and consequence, you don't want every scene to be a downer; you want to keep a delicate mix of positive and negative emotional changes.

How can a complication be good? Well, finding out you have superpowers is awesome, but it might cause you to choose between fighting for justice or being home when you told your mom you'd be there. Getting into the college you dreamed of getting into is a good thing, but when your boyfriend gets waitlisted, are you going to go without him or give up your dream?

Your reader doesn't want one scene of woe after another. I experienced this decades ago, watching the third or fourth season of *ER*, a brilliantly written television show about doctors and nurses. In the first few seasons, they would balance disaster with triumph, but at some point they just started piling on the bad — depression, addiction, divorce, cancer, knife attacks. It fell prey to the melodrama of a soap opera. Disappointment and injustice create empathy between your reader and your character. It makes the reader emotionally invest in your character's success. But, if your protagonist fails every single conflict until the Finale, your reader might not make it there.

Is Your Hero Rising or Falling?

As your hero is put through the promise of the premise, things should be getting steadily better or steadily worse for the character. If you have your Five Tentpole Scenes, you probably already know which way your story is going to go.

Your hero gets superpowers and has gleefully used them to fight the bad guys, and maybe revenge a few past slights. At the midpoint, they feel like everything is finally right in the world.

Or,

Your hero has been framed for theft at work and lost their job. Their husband was depending on that income to finance their new business, and now that has gone bust too. The two quarrel about whose fault it is and breakup. At the Midpoint, your hero is full of anger at everyone and everything in his world and has come up with a plan to rob the company that fired him.

And there's a third option. It's possible that your protagonist's inner struggle is going one way, but their External Goal is going another way.

Your hero gets superpowers, but they have an adverse effect on his psyche, causing paranoia. He keeps using his powers for the good of the city but is losing his friends and family as his psychosis takes over. Up to the Midpoint, he refuses to acknowledge the toll his powers are taking on him.

Or,

After losing his job, your hero has gone to an audition and landed a part in a musical, something they were always too busy to do before. As the Midpoint approaches, your hero is more and more emotionally and creatively fulfilled, but his economic woes have become untenable.

At the Midpoint, you will find that your character is at odds with themselves. Their lives have been upset by the Inciting Incident, and while they have embraced the challenges ahead of them, they haven't really faced up to the flaw that is holding them back. It's time for them to look in the mirror and see themselves for who they really are.

Old Dogs, Old Tricks

One of the principal causes of the conflict you will write in these scenes will be your protagonist's inability to change. Look for scenes where your hero uses their tried-and-true skill set to solve a fresh problem caused by the Inciting Incident. But those old tools aren't going to work, because your character has stepped into a whole new world.

For instance, what if you are writing a comedy, and your main character is a fast-talking lawyer sentenced by a judge to two weeks at a Buddhist retreat where — wait for it — speaking is prohibited? The promise of the premise is straightforward: Your lawyer is going to do everything she can to skirt the rules of the monastery, and when caught, she is going to try to talk her way out of it. This will lead to some funny scenes that will escalate in their ridiculousness.

At the Midpoint, when she looks in the mirror, what will she see? Perhaps someone who hasn't been honest with her loved ones, someone who needs to stop making excuses and say what they really feel. (Completely off topic, but I can't unsee this story now! It's obvious that not only does she reconnect with her family, but she makes an incredible speech in court to defend the abbot of the monastery who has been falsely accused of murdering a mime, who was his rival for the Guinness record for the longest period of silence!)

To recap, these scenes between the Incident and the Midpoint are a series of escalating complications with varied emotional tones. The complications should spring naturally from the main character's initial problem, their flaw, the Inciting Incident, and the consequence of the previous complications. The story should be moving to a high point or a low point, and many of your character's failures should be caused by their inability to learn and grow.

Be aware of the emotional energy of each scene — who's happy, who's unhappy, and how that changes from scene to scene.

What's Happening in Your B Story?

If you have a B Story, you might use it here to hint at the true path for the hero by showing a friend or mentor who is doing it right, or doing it so wrong that it provides a cautionary tale. *My friend Buddy is a poor artist, but they always seem happy.* Or, *My dad is an alcoholic and a constant reminder of what my life will be if I'm not careful.*

You can also plant seeds for how the B Story might collide with the A Story later in the book.

Remember, the B Story can illuminate aspects of your character's inner life and flaw, and now is a good time to lean into that.

The Midpoint Scene Itself

You've led your character down a path. Each scene begins with a wide range of possibilities but ends with your hero being forced to make a difficult choice[x]. "Because of that" choice, the next scene is set up, again with a wide range of possibilities. This continues as your hero rises higher and higher — with a few setbacks here and there — or falls lower and lower (with a triumph or two mixed in).

But there is only so high they can go because their flaw is holding them back, and the Midpoint Tentpole Scene is when it busts out. Remember, it's not when the flaw gets *resolved*, it's when it steps into the limelight.

Raising the Stakes

The middle of your novel should have both an Internal Midpoint, and an External Midpoint. The Internal Midpoint—or Mirror Middle—is about the protagonist's *needs*, and the External Midpoint—or Raise the Stakes scene—is about the protagonist's *wants*.

These two things don't have to happen at the same exact time. Often, the external scene will happen first, causing a crisis of faith in the protagonist that will lead to the **Mirror Moment**. When the plan they thought was going to work suddenly seems hopeless, it is natural for some long-delayed introspection to occur.

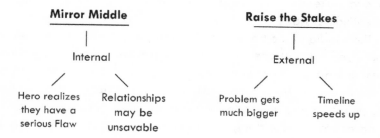

Mirror Middle

Internal

Hero realizes they have a serious Flaw | Relationships may be unsavable

Raise the Stakes

External

Problem gets much bigger | Timeline speeds up

Let's look back on Hazel, our high-speed train designer, and see what we put down for her Midpoint Tentpole.

The Midpoint: *Raise the Stakes: Hazel's first plan fails when a meddling kid breaks an important piece of equipment, and the train picks up speed instead of slowing down. Mirror Moment: The evil chief bureaucrat on the train wrests control of the situation from Hazel and blames her for everyone's imminent death. She absorbs the criticism and abdicates responsibility.*

Does this still work? I think so. It's likely that the "promise of the premise" scenes for Hazel would include outsmarting the bureaucrat in a war of ideas, ingeniously solving a small intervening problem, and bonding with one or two of the kids. The hero would be rising.

When a meddling kid throws everything into chaos, all of Hazel's worst fears will come zooming back. Where she was once able to handily spar with the antagonist, she will crumble at his demands and likely flee to some secluded part of the train. When she looks in the mirror, she will see the lie she has believed — that she needs to control everything in order to keep people safe — but she will learn the *wrong* lesson from it. She will decide that she is useless and worthless.

Hazel will leave the Midpoint in a bad mental place and things will start down a worsening trajectory. The train is going faster, an incompetent jerk is in charge, and children are going to die — exactly the thing Hazel can't bear to have that happen again. You can visualize the coming scenes that will lead to the ultimate choice she will have to make: Can she step back in and save the day by facing and defeating her flaw?

The middle of the book is the hardest part to write. It's the section where you will most often find yourself obsessively checking your word count or adding scenes that don't work because you just want to get to Act Three. The Midpoint Scene is the Tentpole that will prop up your sagging story and give it new intensity and direction. It will be a shot of adrenaline to your story, and it will directly and unmistakably point toward the end of both your *plot* (What enormous obstacle is going to rise up?) and your *story* (How will my hero be forever changed?).

You Are Writing a Book!

Okay, you can't deny it. If you've made it this far, you are officially writing a book! If you've followed my advice, you should in fact be halfway through your first draft!! Wow, you are a writer! You've done what 90% of people who want to write a book never do. What happens next?

Part Three:
The End Is in Sight

Interlude: A Word About Conflict

I have said throughout this book that every scene has to have conflict. Let me tease that apart a bit. It's easy to think that the Three Story Method means every scene has to have an insane, over the top choice and consequence in it, and that those things must be plot related. But there are many kinds of conflict. Instead of physical action, your scene can have an *emotional* conflict and choice, such as deciding what to say in the middle of an argument with a loved one, and the effect that has on their future relationship. Your scene could also have multiple side characters making small demands on the hero, pulling them in different directions and forcing them to decide a course of action. Not all decisions have to be big.

And — this is going to sound weird — not all conflicts and choices are going to have anything to do with the big picture of your story. Sometimes, you can simply manufacture conflict to add movement and tension to your scene. Manufacture conflict? Isn't that cheap theatrics? Not necessarily.

Say you're working on a scene where your hero, Costa, is trying to ask their dad for money to buy tickets to a concert. The concert itself is not the spine of your story, but it's a piece of business that needs to get taken care of to move your plot along. Where is this scene taking place? Is it at the breakfast table, with each character facing each other and making their best argument? That's flat.

Try this instead: Dad has a big meeting but has to take Costa to school first, but Costa is late. Every time Dad tries to get Costa out the door, the kid is talking about some foolish concert. Dad isn't really hearing Costa, and with each minute he is later for work, he is less likely to hear them. Your scene now has not only a conflict of wants — it's not just about what *Costa* wants, it's the conflict of what they *both* want — it is going to escalate as Dad tries harder to get them out the door and Costa sees their chance slipping away. What will Costa choose to do to break through the conflict? Will it work or will it make things worse?

There you go. I have taken a scene and manufactured conflict — just made it up — to make the scene more dynamic. What was the result? Better? Maybe even *more* realistic than what you started with?

As we approach the big Choice in the next chapter, I hope you'll remember the importance of all these little choices.

Chapter 8: The Choice Tentpole Scene

Still here? Maybe I'm making it too easy on you. Well, no more. There's a lot to accomplish in this chapter, and we are going to start by increasing your daily word count to 1000 words a day for 14 days. By this point, if you've actually written 15 to 25 scenes and passed the 20,000-word mark on your manuscript, then you've developed some skills. And importantly, you've silenced your inner critic enough to keep plowing ahead. If you've made it this far, you can make it to the end!

If you are lagging behind, think about why. Are you excited, but just can't make the time in your hectic day to write? That's okay, cut yourself some slack and adjust your calendar. It's okay, really.

Are you just not feeling the story? Take a hard look at your character. Do they have a strong conflict, and are you using them to say something you really believe in? If not, look back at your Pitch and your Five Tentpole Scenes. Maybe this isn't the story you need to be telling. Or, maybe you just need a reminder of where you want to take your story. You can do it! Adjust what needs to be adjusted until you are excited again.

Got the right calendar, got the right story, but still can't get the words down? That's called Resistance, and it's real, and you can beat it. I beat it by writing at least one sentence a day, no matter what. After a day or two, my imagination kicks in and doesn't want to stop after just one sentence, and I've broken through. For you, the answer might be different: an accountability partner can help, or mediation, or a long walk. Don't give up, you can beat it.

Revising Your Character's Goals

An important outcome of your Midpoint should be a shift in your protagonist's goals, both externally and internally. Sometimes the old goal gets replaced, sometimes it just gets tweaked, and sometimes new goals get layered on to the goals that already exist.

Regarding the External Goal, or *wants*, of your character, whatever happened to raise the stakes is going to present a new orientation for action. If we introduce a ticking clock, it may force your protagonist to try an untested shortcut instead of the original plan, or the group may need to split up and be assigned various onerous tasks.

For instance, in our made-up story about Orson and the earthquake, the discovery at the Midpoint that the earthquake was man-made, and that more earthquakes would come soon if no one stopped the madman responsible, will shift Orson's external goal (Because of course Orson is the *only* one capable of stopping the madman!).

The Mirror Moment that occurred for your character means there will also be revisions to her Inner Goal, or *needs*. A character that has recognized, finally, their inner flaw will either come up with a plan to fix it, or come up with a plan to deny and avoid it. Either choice will be the impetus for your next scenes.

What Are Your Next Scenes?

Armed with new goals, what's going to happen now, and how will it lead to our Choice Tentpole Scene? You're the writer, it's up to you. Just remember that you want a strong "Because of That" element of each scene so that it moves logically forward. Here are some of the scenes that you will probably recognize from reading novels and watching movies:

More Escalating, and a Big Win: If your Mirror Moment reinvigorates your protagonist, you might use their new determination to go out there and score a big win over an enormous obstacle. Perhaps they find the villain's lair and disrupt the villain's plan, or perhaps there is an imminent danger to a supporting character that your hero averts. A big win here will make the reader cheer for your hero, but the savvy reader will know that it can't last.

The Antagonist Strikes Back: If your Midpoint was also a high point, it's time for the villain to do some damage and deflate some egos! If your first few scenes after the Midpoint give your hero a big win, it's time for the pendulum to swing the other way.

B Story: Hey, it turns out that other, smaller storyline was connected to your main storyline all along!! (See: Every single Hardy Boys book ever). Now is the time for your hero, with her new perspective after the Mirror Moment, to connect with other characters and decide to work together, forgive each other, etc. Or, the B Story can be the impetus for a Big Win or Big Loss when it collides with the main storyline. You have lots of choices on how to use the B Story. In every case, you need that storyline to teach the main character a lesson, either externally or internally (ideally both) that they will use in Act Three.

Death: Well, it had to happen sometime. It doesn't need to be an actual death. It can be the death of an idea or a relationship, too. Some common deaths are a mentor, a devoted side character, a friendship, a romantic aspiration. Once you look for this scene in books and movies, you will almost always find it. Often it is leading to the Dark Night of the Soul.

The Dark Night of the Soul: This is the scene when your protagonist is at their lowest. They have suffered a serious setback and perhaps a death, and the raised stakes have made it impossible for them to win despite their best efforts. They are ready to quit.

Everything's Not Awesome

You don't have to have every scene that I've listed above. You can mix and match and take the story in any direction you want. The important thing to remember is that almost everything in this section of your book is false.

WHAT??

Everything in this section of your novel is false.

This is a big idea, so let's break it down and talk about character and story first. During your Midpoint Tentpole Scene, your character looked in the mirror and glimpsed their flaw — but they didn't automatically fix that flaw! However, they *did* change their goals, and they decided to either overcome their Flaw, or deny their flaw. This decision sets the course of action for the scenes you're now writing, but in either case, there's a problem.

Old Tools: If your character has had an insight into themselves, and truly wants to change, they are going to try to do that. Unfortunately, they are going to try to do that *with the tools that they already have.* Despite what they have learned, despite what their mentor has tried to teach them. They are either going to misunderstand what they have learned — their "new tools" — or they are going to fall back on old ones. And they are going to fail until they realize this.

In *The Matrix*, the lesson Neo is told but doesn't learn is that "There Is No Spoon." Acknowledging that you are in a construct removes the power of the construct's rules. This is the "new tool" Neo needs. When Neo finally figures this out, he can *actually* see the coding of the construct around him and everything changes — he wins. Until that point, even though he accepts that he is "The One," and that he has exceptional abilities, he gets his ass kicked by Agent Smith.

Not Owning It: If your character glimpses the flaw but denies it, then there can be no real victories, and it will show in the interactions your protagonist has in the next few scenes. He will blame the antagonist for everything that's wrong. He may blame friends for everything that's wrong. He might blame the B Story for keeping him from his goals. Even if he is winning, overcoming obstacles and getting nearer his External Goal, there will be a rot underneath that is going to lead to a fall. The flaw will undermine happiness and satisfaction.

In *About a Boy*, by Nick Hornby, Will is lonely and needs other people. He needs a family. Despite recognizing this in the middle of the book, Will still tries to deny it. He develops a genuine friendship with Marcus, but it is a false win, because deep down, he is unwilling to admit how much he needs that relationship.

The Setup

Now, let's look at this same section of the book from the perspective of External Goals and plot. These scenes of escalating complications, death, big wins, etc., **are still false.** This is the time of misdirection.

In a thriller, these are the scenes where time is running out, the walls are closing in, but the protagonist has a strong External Goal and a plan to get there. (*We just have to reach the control room before Diablo enters the nuclear launch codes!!!!!!!!*)

In a romance, these are the scenes when the protagonist has

screwed up their chance, but they have a plan to write a sonnet/recreate the loved one's childhood home in Legos/hold a boom box over their head/etc. There are a lot of escalating conflicts that try to stop the hero from pulling the scheme off, but the hero overcomes them all!

These scenes are false because the hero *thinks* progress is being made, but in fact, things are getting worse. When they burst into the control room, Diablo has a hostage! Or, the police come and arrest our hero for disturbing the peace by playing his boom box too loud.

If you want your upcoming Third Act to be interesting, surprising, and memorable, then something completely unexpected will happen during the Finale of the book. Something your character doesn't suspect, and if you are lucky (and clever) then something your reader doesn't suspect either. These false scenes will help set that up.

Sell It

These scenes may end up being misdirection, but you must write them with as much conviction as any of the other scenes. And you must use them wisely — to deepen friendships, reinforce your theme, highlight the character's flaw, and lay the groundwork for the rest of your novel.

The Final Act

These six to eight scenes after the midpoint should also take your plot from Act Two to Act Three. That shift occurs when the falsehoods are revealed, and the new path is decided upon. This act break should feel obvious.

This new path is going to lead the protagonist fairly quickly to the Choice Tentpole Scene. Your reader will be ready — once they know what the ultimate challenge is — for you to get there without delay.

Whether it's storming the castle, setting a trap for the killer, or devising the grand romantic gesture, don't dawdle. Use a few scenes to show the final plan coming together, right up to the point of unavoidable crisis, when the protagonist must face their flaw if they have any hope of succeeding.

The Choice Tentpole Scene

Guess what? It's time for your protagonist to find out that everything they thought they knew was wrong. Their grand plan is in shambles. Everything's not awesome.

Some made up examples:

Romance: Your hero's love sonnet is brilliant and goes viral on the internet, but it turns out the love interest is secretly married and has been all along!!!

Fantasy: After months of sacrifice and searching, they find the talisman that will give your hero the power to defeat the evil Grim. Guess what? It doesn't work.

Mystery: You've finally found the secret hideout of the woman responsible for the string of grisly murders. You bust in to find her... dead on the floor in a pool of blood!

The result of these new truths should be a *new* problem. A huge problem. That's the bad news.

The good news is you will make it clear to the protagonist what the solution to the problem is. Yay!

The bad news is the solution is going to require a choice. Not just a choice, but The Choice, and that choice is going to be hard. In fact, it's going to be *impossible* unless your hero overcomes their flaw.

A recent television example that I'd like to recommend is *Squid Game*, a Korean show that I only watched because people said it was outrageous (It is both outrageous and bloody, so be warned). It is also a master class in using the Three Story Method to generate impossible choices for its protagonists, and each impossible choice both reveals something about the characters' inner selves and connects us to them on a deeply empathetic level.

Checking In on Your Choice

If you've been taking these lessons seriously—and I hope you have—you should already have an idea for your Choice Scene written down. It should be evident in your Logline and your Pixar Pitch. It's time to take those out, dust them off, and see if your Choice Tentpole Scene is still on target.

Let's reach back to Chapter 3, and our story about Samir and Ginni. What did I have down for The Choice and The Finale for that story, about a man who pretended to be his famous brother to date the woman he fell for?

> **The Choice:** *Samir returns to New York for the publication of a series of profiles he did while in Ukraine. Will he find Ginni and apologize?*

> **The Climax:** *Samir avoids Ginni, who is still mad until she sees the work Samir has done while he's been away. She seeks him out. He apologizes and they live happily ever after.*

This is kind of lame, no? What was Samir's flaw? Cynicism and a misplaced sense of injustice. Does this crisis choice give us a chance to show Samir facing those flaws? Maybe. If he realizes everything has been his fault, and *not* that he has been the victim of injustice, then he has a chance to give a genuine apology that isn't tinged with cynicism.

But we could also try to strengthen it. How about this?

The Choice: When Samir finds out Ginni is about to publish a scathing and bitter review of Samir's new work, he must decide whether to retaliate or to endure the critical review.

The Finale: As their argument spirals out of control, Samir realizes he has caused Ginni's pain, and that while her revenge was unkind, it was not unjustified. He breaks through her defenses and apologizes. She admits that his new work is great. They agree to start over.

Is it better? I think so, because it focuses more tightly on Samir's flaws. The choice as I present it in this second version is actually *between* his two flaws, cynicism (I should have known this would come back to bite me) and injustice (It's not right for Ginni to torch my work, I'm going to fight back and ruin her reputation as well).

This is a no-win choice for Samir. However, it gives the opportunity for a third choice. As he writes a rebuttal, he realizes it would be better to confront Ginni in person. Their argument is the climactic scene of the book, and during it Samir can see her humanity, and see that he hurt her terribly by lying to her. Sometimes our first Choice gives a chance for a second Choice or action, and in this case, Samir discards his cynicism and realizes he deserved what he got for lying. He overcomes both of his flaws. Ginni hasn't been a saint in all this either, and so if she admits her mistakes, too, they can start over and have a chance at an honest relationship.

Now it's time for you to look at *your* planned Choice Tentpole Scene.

- Does it work?
- Is it an extremely hard choice?
- Is it a choice only the protagonist can make?
- Is it a choice that relates to their inner flaw?
- Is it a choice that will change them forever?

If any of your answers are no, then you've got to revise your idea for the scene. If *all* your answers are yes, then you're ready. Go to it!

Review

Moving from the middle toward the Third Act and the Choice Tentpole Scene, there's a lot going on. Here are some things to remember:

- You should feel a sense of direction and motion after the Midpoint Choice Scene. If you don't, back up and work on that section again; otherwise, you are in for an unhappy slog.
- Your Hero needs to *think* they know the answers, what they have to do to reach their goal. But they don't.
- Add a whiff of death. Whether it's a real death, or just something forever lost, your hero needs help making a break from the past, and a death can help with that.
- Make your Choice big, meaningful, and irreversible.

Chapter 9. The Finale Tentpole Scene(s)

Choices have consequences. The biggest choice has the biggest consequence.

You already have your Finale in mind, don't you? I know when I write, I start with the Inciting Incident and the Finale, and then try to figure out all the messy middle bits. Sometimes things change as you write, though, and you'd be a fool to stick with your original idea if you've come up with something better. Outlines are meant to be flexible.

What the Choice Has Changed

Your Finale Tentpole Scene will follow close on the heels of your Choice Tentpole Scene. In some ways, the Finale is much less important than the Choice, because it's the Choice Scene that focuses on the Internal Goal and the flaw, and as I've said so many times, that's where the authentic story lies. **It's your character's emotional journey that we invest the reader in.**

That said, readers still expect you to come through with an outstanding Finale, am I right? You've got to pay off everything you set up, and you've got to do it in a way that delights the reader.

Note that your Finale can be several scenes, probably *will* be several scenes, especially in a thriller or fantasy. You've spent the entire book building up to it, so your Finale might need a bit of extra room! But don't make it *too* long — once we have reached the emotional payoff, it's easy for a reader to get bored with even the most spectacular spectacle. I'm sure you can think of some blockbuster movies guilty of this.

Can your Choice and your Finale overlap or happen at the same time? Yes, they can. The longer you make your Finale, the more likely that they will. Or, that your Finale will have a "False Finale" that sparks the Choice, which then leads to a bigger Finale.

In *The Silence of the Lambs*, the Choice Tentpole Scene happens when Clarisse decides she is going to do the right thing for the victims and investigate a lead, even though the FBI threw her off the case and warned away. She must choose between her career and her desire to save lives. Once she makes that choice, the Finale unfolds when she enters the killer's house.

In *Avengers: Endgame*, however, the Choice happens (at least for one of the character arcs) when Tony Stark uses the Infinity Stones even though he knows they will kill him. This choice is the culmination of a long journey from selfishness to selflessness, and it happens near the end of a very long Finale.

The fallout of the Choice is going to change some things:

Agency: On a character level, defeating the flaw is going to give your character more confidence and even more agency. Up to this point, you've been trying to make your protagonist active rather than reactive. Now, you *must* double down on that. Your character has already made the hardest choice, now they're going to be more decisive and forceful in dealing with the fallout. When I do a developmental edit for a new author, lack of agency in the Finale is one of the biggest issues I find, every time. Your hero can't barely escape with their life by running really fast when the volcano erupts. Your hero needs to be the only one who knows the escape route because of an important decision they made earlier in the story, and they have to be the one to lead others to safety.

New Tools: Now that your character has faced their flaw, they should have a new way of winning. We talked earlier about trying to solve new problems with old tools. Now, finally, the hero admits that the old tools will never work again, and they look for new solutions. Keeping this in mind will help you create original and surprising finales.

Combining B Story: The subplot that expanded your character's inner journey, or showed a nuance of your theme, should now fold into your main story, if it hasn't already. While her flaw still hampered your hero, there was a friction between the two stories. That friction should now resolve.

When crafting your Finale, keep these changes in mind, and use them to make your Finale pop.

Surprising but Inevitable

I love that term, *Surprising but inevitable*. As far as I can tell, it was invented by Shawn Coyne, the creator of Story Grid. It's an important phrase to keep in mind. It refers to the need for your story to make logical sense, but also to be unexpected.

In *Wired for Story*, by Lisa Cron, she explains that readers' brains work hard to figure out what happens next in a story. Your brain loves to do that. It loves to say, *Aha! I knew it!!*

You know this, but what you might not know is that there is something your brain loves to do *even more* when reading a story. It loves to say *Wow! I should have known! Boy, I didn't see that coming!!* In other words, your reader loves to be tricked, but only if the clues were there for the reader to have figured it out for themselves. If the resolution of the plot comes out of nowhere, and wasn't set up beforehand, then they are going to throw your book against the wall. Hard.

Thus, surprising but inevitable.

I hate to use *Star Wars* again. So many writing craft books use it, but they use it because so many people have seen it, and it follows all the rules of storytelling I've been shouting at you all this time.

So, just look at the Finale of *Star Wars*. After a horrific battle with ten zillion tie fighters, Luke is one of only two rebel fighters left. It's his turn to shoot a missile down the tiny little ventilation shaft. At the urging of Kenobi's ghost, he turns off his targeting computer and uses The Force instead.

- **Hero Agency?** Check. Luke is deciding on his own.

- **New Tools?** Check. Luke is an excellent marksman but decides to use The Force.

- **B Story?** Check. In this first movie, The Force is really a side story to the main plot of saving the princess.

- **Surprising but inevitable?** Check. What was all that Force stuff for if it wasn't going to come back at the end? (Han Solo popping up at the Finale was also inevitable, but not all that surprising).

When you work on your second draft, you should look at the Conflict, Choice, and Consequence of each scene and ask, *Is it surprising?* Are there set-ups and payoffs, and are they logically grounded but unexpected? It's one of my favorite parts of editing, because you can go back and lay clever clues for a big payoff, even if you didn't think of the big payoff until halfway through writing the book. Your reader only reads in one direction, from beginning to end, and they think you only write in one direction, too. But you don't have to. Editing helps you look like a genius.

Supersize It

But back to your surprising but inevitable Finale. Take out your outline if you have one, or just your Five Tentpole Scenes, if that's all you've got, and look at your Finale.

Is it surprising? Does it sync up with the clues and expectations you've laid out in the book so far?

It doesn't? Well then, using all you've learned so far, take twenty minutes to sit down and figure out a Finale that is more in line with your character's emotional journey. Create a massive problem that they are the best person to solve because of what they have just learned about themselves. A problem that they could not have solved with their former beliefs. Excellent. Write that down.

Now, look at your Finale, either your new one or your original one if it still holds up. Take out a blank piece of paper and, in one paragraph, describe your Finale, expanding your one sentence description to two or three sentences.

Now, below that, I want you to describe FIVE MORE FINALES that would fit in with the plot and story that you have written up to this point. Make each one BIGGER and CRAZIER than the one before it.

Wait, what? You worked so hard on your Five Tentpole Scenes. Why do I want you to throw this one out, and why am I talking in ALL CAPS?

Here's why.

When you are looking at the arc and flaw of your character, some great ideas are going to jump out at you. The problem is these ideas jump out so quickly *because they are familiar to you.* Well, guess what, if they are familiar to you, then they are going to be familiar to your reader as well.[xi] We don't want familiar; we want surprising. And, as I've said before, what seems over the top to you will not seem quite as extreme to your reader. You have more room to up the wow factor than you think, so go ahead and up it.

Please, take half an hour and do this exercise. It's possible you will stick with your first idea, and that's okay. One, that idea might be great. With my first novel, it was a *particular* Finale Scene that first popped into my head. I reverse engineered the entire novel to lead up to that point. There was no way in hell I was going to change it at that point. And it worked. Don't throw out your idea just for the sake of throwing it out.

The second reason it's okay to keep your first idea is that this is still your First Draft! If you stick around for my next book, *Edit Your Novel: First Draft to Final Draft,* then I'm going to make you do that exercise again anyway.

But, if you do it now, and a brilliant new idea pops into your head, you'll have saved yourself a lot of time. So give it a go. I'll wait.

Yes, five alternate Finales. Don't just do three.

Still waiting.

Okay. Great job. Now pick the one you like the best. Or show the five choices to five people and see which one they like best. But choose.

Go write your Finale Scene or Scenes now. Be sure your protagonist is using their new tools and new outlook to solve the problem they couldn't solve before. Be sure your antagonist is trying to stop them but fails because *they* never changed during the novel, or they changed for the worse. An enlightened hero should be able to see the antagonist's unhealed flaw and exploit it in the Finale.

I can't wait to see what you come up with.

The Finale Tentpole Exercise in Action

I know this exercise seems extreme, and maybe unnecessary, so I thought I'd do it here for you, so you can see what it might look like, and what it might accomplish for you. Let's go back to our friend Dieter, the detective with the gambling problem.

Finale Scene #1.

Dieter is in the club with Armand, about to close the illegal deal, when the cops burst in. When the crime boss takes aim at Dieter's Captain, Dieter steps in and shoots the boss. Despite being a hero, he is still arrested for his involvement in the crime syndicate.

Finale Scene #2

Dieter is in the club when the cops burst in. As the police captain and Armand face off, Dieter steps between them, a gun in each hand. He must choose which one to side with. He chooses the captain. Armand shoots at him and hits him in the shoulder. Dieter shoots back at Armand and kills him.

Finale Scene #3

When the police burst into the club, it turns out Armand has been their informant all along, and he tells them Dieter and Marlene are the culprits. Marlene pulls a gun and when she tries to shoot Armand, Dieter intervenes, saving Armand but accidentally killing Marlene.

Finale Scene #4

Armand, Dieter, and Marlene are in the back room of the club when they hear the police rush in. Armand accuses Dieter of selling him out and pulls a gun and threatens Marlene, knowing Dieter is in love with her. Dieter draws and shoots, killing Armand as police rush in, shooting and killing Dieter in the confusion.

Finale Scene #5

As the club is raided, a fire starts and soon the club is engulfed in flames. Dieter and Marlene make a run for the back door, but they are confronted by Armand, who is furious that Dieter has stolen Marlene from him. There's a gunfight, and Armand and Marlene are killed. Dieter has a chance to escape, but instead he returns to the club to help get injured police officers out of the burning building. He confesses his crimes and addictions and is put on probation pending review. He also enrolls in Gamblers Anonymous.

Ooh, should Dieter die at the end? Should there be a version where he and Marlene escape to embrace a life of crime? You don't have to stop at five scenarios. Keep going until you find the perfect one.

Review

Your Finale Tentpole Scene:

- Needs to make logical sense
- Needs to pay off earlier set-ups
- Needs to relate to the character's flaw
- Needs to be as intense and emotional as you can make it
- Needs the hero to do something she never could have on page one
- Needs to be surprising but inevitable

Chapter 10. The Aftermath

Holy guacamole, you did it!

How do you feel? Excited? Queasy?

Let me guess: *It's total crap! Your book is terrible!!*

Maybe, maybe not. Don't let that bother you. You've planned a novel by creating a character and generating your Five Tentpole Scenes, and now you've written those scenes, and all the scenes in between!

Congratulations. But guess what? You're not quite done yet. There are still a few scenes left. Scenes I refer to as **The Aftermath**.

These are the scenes that show us the consequences of the Choice and the Finale. Your character made an impossible choice, one they can never undo. How has that changed their world? It's time to tell us.

Don't make these scenes too long or write too many of them.

It's a New World

Do take enough time to show the reader what has changed because of the journey your hero has taken. If you remember back to the opening chapters of your book, there is something wrong with your hero's life even *before* the Inciting Incident. Now, that problem should be gone, or be easily handled in the last scenes of your story. What is life going to be like for your hero from now on? Is *everything* fixed, or will she still have challenges ahead?

Setting Up a Series

These scenes are also great for setting up a series. You can create a new problem for your protagonist that is outlined here in these final scenes. Be careful, though, there are some definite dos and don'ts you want to keep in mind.

Don't fail to resolve the main conflict of your book and promise that resolution in the next book. All you are really doing is taking a big story and breaking it in half. Your reader will be annoyed.

Do open up a new, unresolved conflict earlier in the book if possible. This is sometimes better done in revisions. Try to avoid throwing the reader a curve ball at the very last moment.

Do use references to incidents in the protagonist's past to set up a conflict in the future. You may have referenced a falling out with a parent as a reason for your protagonist's flaw. In a future book, you could bring that parent in as a character that sets the plot in motion.

Don't go into too much depth about the new problem. Your reader is still digesting the consequences of the Choice and Finale. You want to let them marinate in your brilliance before you pull their attention in a different direction.

What's Next?

After writing "The End," it's time to celebrate, of course. Let's look at what you've accomplished!

- You've created a unique protagonist with a strong, distinctive **Voice** and a deep personal **Flaw**.

- You've created an antagonist that perfectly contrasts with your protagonist and has their own **wants** and **needs** that will conflict with the wants and needs of your hero.

- You've created key supporting characters that will help drive your hero forward or hold her back.

- You've used the protagonist's flaw to create an **emotional journey** for them, by creating a big **choice** that will leave them forever changed.

- You've used that information to create an Inciting Incident, a Point of No Return, a Midpoint, a Choice, and a Finale. Your **Five Tentpole Scenes.**

- You've planned out scenes to fill in the spaces between those Five Tentpole Scenes.

- You've written between 50,000 and 100,000 words!!!

- You've created a **Finale** to your story that is surprising but inevitable.

The next step is NOT to start drafting query letters to agents. Sorry to tell you. In fact, I wouldn't even recommend showing your work to anyone. Why? Because what you've written is a *rough draft*. If you remember, I actually referred to it as a *Vomit Draft*. Be proud, be very proud, but the next step is to sit down, roll up your sleeves, and write your second draft. And your third and fourth. Then, you'll be ready to introduce your amazing book to other readers.

If you've found this book helpful, I hope you will pick up volume two of this series: *Edit Your Novel: First Draft to Final Draft.*

Until then, congratulations, and happy revising!!

Join me at AuthorHelp.net for publishing information, tips, and other helpful resources.

Sources

When I wrote this book I tried to pull together everything I've learned from the last ten years of helping authors get their words into the world. However, I also included many things I've learned from particular voices in the publishing world. Here are some of them, in no particular order:

- Joanna Penn, author and host of The Creative Penn Podcast
- Jeff Elkins, host of The Dialogue Doctor Podcast
- Lisa Cron, the author of Wired for Story and other books.
- J. Thorn and Zach Bohannon, podcasters and authors of *The Three Story Method*
- Shawn Coyne, author of *The Story Grid*
- Matt Bird, author of *The Secrets of Story*
- Rachael Herron, author and host of the How Do You Write Podcast
- Donald Maas, author of *The Emotional Craft of Fiction*
- Seth Godin, host of the Akimbo Podcast
- James Scott Bell, author of *Write Your Novel from the Middle*

...and many others!

Endnotes

[i] Wired for Story by Lisa Cron, 2012
[ii] Three Story Method: Writing Scenes by J.Thorn, 2022
[iii] The Story Grid by Shawn Coyne, 2015
[iv] Save the Cat by Blake Snyder, 2005
[v] The War of Art by Steven Pressfield, 2012
[vi] Three Story Method: Writing Scenes by J. Thorn, 2022
[vii] Wired for Story by Lisa Cron, 2012
[viii] The Secrets of Story by Matt Bird, 2016
[ix] Save the Cat by Blake Snyder, 2005
[x] Take off Your Pants by Libby Hawker, 2015
[xi] The Three Story Method by Thorn and Bohannon, 2022

CPSIA information can be obtained
at www.ICGtesting.com
Printed in the USA
JSHW061015251022
32082JS00001B/5